**THE PACIFIC NORTHWEST POETRY SERIES**

LINDA BIERDS, GENERAL EDITOR

## THE PACIFIC NORTHWEST POETRY SERIES

2001  John Haines  *For the Century's End*
2002  Suzanne Paola  *The Lives of the Saints*
2003  David Biespiel  *Wild Civility*
2004  Christopher Howell  *Light's Ladder*
2005  Katrina Roberts  *The Quick*
2006  Bruce Beasley  *The Corpse Flower*
2007  Nance Van Winckel  *No Starling*
2008  John Witte  *Second Nature*
2009  David Biespiel  *The Book of Men and Women*
2010  Christopher Howell  *Dreamless and Possible*

# DREAMLESS AND POSSIBLE

POEMS NEW AND SELECTED

**CHRISTOPHER HOWELL**

**UNIVERSITY OF WASHINGTON PRESS** SEATTLE AND LONDON

*DREAMLESS AND POSSIBLE*, THE NINTH VOLUME IN THE

PACIFIC NORTHWEST POETRY SERIES, IS PUBLISHED WITH

THE GENEROUS SUPPORT OF CYNTHIA LOVELACE SEARS.

© 2010 by the University of Washington Press
Printed in the United States of America
Design by Ashley Saleeba
16 14 12 11 10   5 4 3 2 1

Interior illustrations are by David Luckert; reproduced by permission of the artist.
© David Luckert.

University of Washington Press
P.O. Box 50096, Seattle, WA 98145 U.S.A.
www.washington.edu/uwpress

Library of Congress Cataloging-in-Publication Data
Howell, Christopher.
Dreamless and possible : poems new & selected / by Christopher Howell.
    p. cm. — (The Pacific Northwest poetry series)
ISBN 978-0-295-99012-5 (hardback : alk. paper)
I. Title.
PS3558.O897D74 2010
811'.54—dc22          2010007789

The paper used in this publication is acid-free and 90 percent recycled from at least 50 percent
post-consumer waste. It meets the minimum requirements of American National Standard for
Information Sciences—Permanence of Paper for Printed Library Materials, ANSI Z39.48-1984.∞

*This book is for Barbara and Evan*
*and in memory of Emma*

# CONTENTS

# DREAMLESS AND POSSIBLE

## NEW POEMS

There is no life that does not rise
melodic from scales of the marvelous.

To which our grief refers.
—*Robert Duncan*

## DANCERS

The bee drifts from the lily and the lily fronds
bow. Some color is involved, changeably
according to breeze and shadow.
By the lake people are doing something
with a barbecue or a boat
while others do something with plates.

Some of those I love have left the world.

If the sun continues and the blue sky burns
and the sea reaches into itself almost lazily
for food and the arithmetic of what looks like
grace (until it kills you), what use my grieving
hope? Something blue-black soughs in me
like a storm of ancient invitation and regard.

But some of those I love have left the world.

Any moment heralds will announce the feast
and dancers, draped in tiny bells,
will step and turn along the twilit shore
and who will hear them, and who will rise
from sleep or death to dance among them
the dance of the bee who returns alone

into his own country?

## BURNING BUSH

I think of my father on his knees, hammering
at the floor of what would become
the new bedroom
as we, on our knees, prayed to the campfire
we were trying to kindle
in the field that bordered the dirt road.

With our lips like little valentines we leaned close
and huffed softly, just as Roy Rogers had shown us
a hundred times, and sat back, pouring
our imaginary coffee, when
*boom:* there it was! the burning bush!
Scotch broom exploding like the breath
of God Almighty and so hot! our cowboy hats
flew off. The whole field: just *whoosh!*
No time to save the horses, Tex, better run for it!
as my father ran
then, dragging three-hundred feet of strung-together hose,
yelling, "Get out of there! Get out!"
just minutes ahead of the fire truck and screaming
neighbors.

I remember Cecil Morris tripping in the tail
ends of his armload of garden hoses
and sprawling full out as though worshipping the Fire Department
just then connecting to the new hydrant
on the corner, first one planted out so far from town.
They blasted the blaze to smoldering char
then assaulted the whole field with shovels and axes,
taking no prisoners.

My father,
covered in soot, half soaked and breathing hard,
stood before me and said, "Give Me the Matches."
I handed them over.
The crowd looked on with approving sternness.

This is it, I thought, they'll hang us for sure
this time.
I looked at the sky and the huge firemen.
What would Heaven be like?
My father put his hand on my shoulder
as though he already knew.

# ANOTHER LETTER TO THE SOUL

I think you are among the flowers
that spill from walls and urge
the hummingbirds to drink and drink
from their fantastic hair.
Each day I believe more firmly
in this life of yours among the brilliance
that thrusts and blooms on into the blue
foyer of the sun. In this way
I understand my own flowering
as your shadow left advisedly
against the noise of loneliness
which would otherwise be your absence.
God love you more than dust, I pray
to the fireball lastness of descending light,
and keep you steady while the world
sways on its pins.
Shattered rock and silver rings, music
of the vibrant wood itself: how much matters
and by how intricate a moon?
I have put off from shore to think these
things, the wind right aft, the sail in blossom
toward the godly open certainty
that you are with me still
and joyful
as the small, doomed, brightly painted boat
that I must be.

# THE RADIO IS PLAYING STRAUSS

which always conjures images of ballrooms
full of smiling SS officers in dress greys
twirling with willowy frauleins afloat
in clouds of taffeta and silk.

There's a war on, but they're winning it and who cares
how it started. Emeralds, diamonds, beautifully
designed and manufactured weapons, the official
distaste for kindness, all of it

waltzes gaily into the spring of 1941
and the pleasant prospect of Moscow
by June, when the real cleansing
can begin. They dance and dance, thinking of all that

space, an almost infinite ballroom buried
in three-four time, and time itself absolutely
their protector for a thousand German years, which,
it turns out, are shorter than Allied years.

When the music ends
and they lead the women out to spiffy black staff cars
driven by heel-clicking non-coms and roll off
to more intimate entertainments, the orchestra members

will be packing up their instruments, grabbing
a tired smoke, maybe, outside the stage door
where night is fingering the bricks and little
splinters of glass that seem still to be everywhere

glinting, like tiny prayers or gold
fillings, in what is left of the light.

# TIME TRAVEL

The moon is up on its hind legs
over the shed.
Some dogs from up around Montavilla
announce their moonstruck praise
of that lovely light/dark contrast
which informs the soul, though perhaps
these brothers of Judas have no souls,
as Aquinas insisted.

I'm in the grade school parking lot
firing a rubber-coated baseball
against the brick face of the gymnasium,
each pitch disappearing like a train
into a tunnel
and coming back like a spear.

I reach back for more power as the stars
turn and the dogs whine in circles
and lie down, their contracts fulfilled.
I have the sense that someone far away
is watching as the phantom batsmen
shiver in their shoes and swat the air
like the blind clutching at butterflies
or wind.

This someone wants to say his nights
are not the same as mine, though moon
and stars are always what they were.
He's different and strangely sad.
He wants to say, "Throw harder, the great
crowds of Heaven cheer you on and on
and will never forget your ignorant beauty."

# THE HOT CORNER
*—for Joe Millar*

Across from Watts Automotive and Driveline
I sit drinking coffee and watching the same
unmarked cop car cruise by
for the sixth time. Sniffy
and dangerously relaxed, the cops inside
radiate the cool fuck you anger
of the third baseman when the right
handed pull hitter steps up and everyone
in the park knows where the ball
is going. They want meat
of some kind. They smell dope and money
calls them like bad luck or the exact thing
you didn't want to happen.
Not that they wouldn't help me if I didn't
look too much a fool who could just
sit over there and shut up, sir, while we do
our job. Not that they wouldn't
roust me out of my car and fling me face down
over the steaming hood if it were late
enough and in just the right
neighborhood, my hair too
something, my car too low or too red, and they
sick to death of waiting for that
blistering line drive.

# THE DREAM OF '64

Sometimes I feel alone as I was the summer of '64, working at Kodak,
driving a Renault that wouldn't
start without the assistance of a hill—one time, up in the Cascades,
the only hill available was
a boat ramp and I drove right into the lake, which did not help
the car's electrical problems.
It was the summer I pitched for that disastrous semi-pro team
from Lents
and me and Johnsrud were the only players who could throw,
hit, or field.
Years later the coach, a Catholic, told me anyone who watched
those games
should get time off in Purgatory. Thanks be to God, we played at night.
After the games
I would drive to the top of Mt. Scott where there were no houses
yet
and sit on the hood of that car to watch stars and the pulsing
passage of satellites, both
"ours" and "theirs," and listen for what might matter or
might speak.
In hopes she would "forget about" me over the summer, my girlfriend
had been sent off to California,
a thing parents did back then when the boy clearly wanted only "one thing"
and was in other ways undesirable.
She wrote long chatty letters that would have depressed a saint,
so the gambit
seemed to be working. My parents and most of the adults I knew
were so deep
in their dream, they spoke mostly in movements of a dance
that seemed both somber and immense.
And now I am the dreamer, shimmering, everyone I care for
purling at an intimate

remove, stopped clocks moving, planetary, placed in this steepening life
like something that won't start
by a God who is rumored to have made all things as they are, even
this interstellar baseball
we call home, sailing high over the blue fence of its own breath
into that loneliness
all around and inside us like nothing and all things, like the mysterious
glowing
emptiness of love itself.
"Open Me First" it said, at Christmas time, on those boxes the Kodak
Brownie Hawkeye
cameras always came in.
Open, say cheese, and look in for the sign. Steady now. The light has to be
just right. Notice that
through this lens, all distance is enormous. If we wake like this and find
ourselves
gone, at least
we'll have these pictures. But who is the boy in this one?

## AT MIDNIGHT

by a bridge slippery with starry
incandescence
I could not make sense of her
breasts. Their gleaming self-containment
satisfied and mysterious
in the dark.
Loons, veiled in the hair-like fall
of willow boughs, gave us their soft soprano
trill. Don't tell me you care how many times
I touched those rosy pearls
and the other in its beauteous nest,
if I did.
Some days are not for counting. Memory's rooms
are sleepless with solitude and a grieving
gladness. Who knows why
they open and there is a starlit bridge
and someone you loved, her nakedness and absence
like clouds and rain on the dark far shore.

## I REMEMBER THE QUEEN'S REVIEW
## OF THE NATO FLEET

Blue sea and the blue sky blue above
the grey and white ships. We stood

topside in ranks to watch the ritual of her
passage, just as Anaximander and Archilochus

and Cochran in the time of Pitt the Younger
must have stood in stiff acknowledgment

of whatever powers commanded them
to lay their lives before the god

of ceremony, wisdom's lost brother
sneaking in a window while the parents sleep

like angels at a blackjack table, knowing
the outcome, betting on loss to make it right.

It was forty years ago I saw the white queen slide
past, and thought, "I will remember myself

seeing this." But what I see now is Portsmouth
like a slightly shabby diadem around the bay

where the great fleet breathes and bows
to history's interminable menace

and the queen in white lace like a bride
nods as she goes by.

# TIGER TIGER

## 1

I dreamed the earth was empty of all
but tigers and a few hapless survivors
of the human disaster. The tigers sang,
*La Boheme* I think it was, as they hunted
and devoured us. I lay by the river,
hardly daring to move my eyes.
Their voices were so beautifully like the light
on summer mornings and their fur so rich
with softness, it was not easy to remember
the screaming or the sad prayers of those
dragged from hiding and broken in the tigers'
melodious jaws. When it was my turn, suddenly
I became my father and all threat
flew up like doves into green mansions
of the moon where the tigers were women
who loved us, in spite of what we were.

## 2

I told no one. I was compelled
to keep the light clean of repetition
and remorse. And in the wholly strange music
of women I flew with both selves
darkened by fulfillment, with all my wings
joyful and asleep. I was given a single
moment for this, there among the dazzling
transmigrations, and it went on and on.
What could suffering matter, at last?
I loved my father, his face, delicate
as a spirit offering its only life.
I loved my self,
though I did not know its name.

## DUST TO DUST

Over the hill the many birds fly, tilted, sometimes
singing, I imagine.

Shuffling, intentless, listening, I raise
little questions and statements of dust, the very kind
my mother has become, circling up through
maple boughs and blowing away to join the birds
or find what sky might mean
by its exact shades of presence and bright blue.

Candle flames. Trees, bent rivers of air. Far off, someone
singing "Abide with Me."

What will I do now? The game is Here Comes the Measureless
Dust, to which I offer the matter of my contrition
and the matter of love joined in lilies and pears
and sorrows finding their way
as we all must do.

Soon rain will come again, its music
brother to what shines, its crows perfect in their slanting
disposition, its windows open and the smell of rain and dust
rising.

The nature of blessing is so strange, a small dull stone
picked up by sheerest whim that you might possess the merest
glimmer of its secret name and place it
in whatever cup the dark provides
and hold God blameless
because of this.

## HOME IS THE SAILOR

Rounding the corner, sea bag heavy
on my shoulder, I was
every man who ever came home
from war. And, indeed, they—
gathered at the big front window—
saw me knowing this, taking on the joy
of the Roman legionnaire when, after 25 years
on the ramparts in Gaul, the farm
came into view and the wife
and grown children ran speechless
toward him up the road.
I had done my duty, so to speak.
The great engines soaked in blood
slept in the distance
of my shoes. An iron encirclement
left the houses of my fingers
and hair and I entered the shadows
of strangers whose language was tinsel
and glass goblets overflowing, whose soft hands
touched me like morning in another time.
Birdsong and plums opened their invisible books for me
who had become that no one
standing beside himself
while history shook its head.
Give me a moment, I said, give me
a hand with this bag of voices and bones.
I didn't care
what mattered. All through my body, in the dark
totality of my life, a Confederate soldier
sat down by the fire
and slept.

# FACE

Black window in the side
of a barn, one of those
where they keep winter
when they aren't using it,
shows me my face.
It's a kind
of snowstorm face, frozen blue pools
in a landscape of brown and grey grass.
Below some of the larger hills you can see
braided trails where the snow has melted
and run down into the valleys.
And high up there's a path
where someone drove toward the forest
with a plough or something
trailing out behind.

Accustomed to black windows
and barns, its look
says it doesn't hope for much,
though it would like to find a certain weather
going on inside it. So, it craves sunlight;
why not (let feet have the actual snow
if they're so wild about slogging on)?

It went to sea once, of course, and came home
not quite
like a cloud's remorse above a slough.
Nevertheless, it is my oldest friend, a face maybe
you'd know, a weary
and brotherlike garden-gate kind of face
half ready to think it knows you, too.
A face that's seen a lot of rain

come over the hill, a face
that came over the hill itself and found
the valley of strangers
who said, "Look at that face! I know that
countryside. Some of us lived there
before the war."

## LETTING THINGS GO

So now I'm thinking about mushrooms,
their curious smell and lightness,
about the great adventure of not knowing
exactly which were poison
and which would get you off like Flash Gordon
in a purple car, about how we wandered pastures
plucking and praying for the wild ride
that seldom came.

And in that connection I have to think
of 1974, Montana Bill and I driving all the way
to Manzanillo in a Dodge van
to present my manuscript of poems to
John Muir Publications
at their annual conference and drug fest.
After days of negotiation, it was agreed
I would read to the twenty or more principal mavens
of the group, including Muir himself, and they
would decide.

We gathered around a huge table out
under the stars
and I opened my manuscript . . .
but *first*, Muir said, we should "get into the mood"
and began to load his pipe with a weed
and *Psilocybe mexicana* mixture which everyone
smoked until their eyes were huge, pulsing zeros.

Then I read. It was like hollering
into a vat of butter, like singing to Martians
about the stock exchange.

When, after three hundred years, I finished,
they nodded into themselves, looked around
and went off toward the beach.
Two days later the managing editor collared me
and said, "Well, they thought I should talk to you
because we're about the same height. So,
it's like this, we know you're a good poet
and we'd really like to help you out, but
you're into holding onto things

and we're into *letting things go*."

## JUNG DOUBTS

It may not be possible to go deeper, beyond
or beneath anything but birds and their
little thoughts feathered among the leaves.
Perhaps we're stuck in the bruise of broad day
with its donkey cart clang and silence like a choir
of gestures
or an aerial view of schoolgirls spilling from a school.
Perhaps we will open the inner door and find no stairs
or an immense frozen stone pointing at its old friend
the moon of our echo
going round and round with little trays of sweets
remembered and given
casually
in the service of regret.
And though the deep rooms knock and sometimes sing
we can't help thinking what if our minds aren't really
anything? What if no one's there, dear lady
who lifts her arms up to our own, dear contused old man
whose tears run in the blackened street
we climb, convinced the beloved is behind us and our lives
before us in a shadow of the shadow of the light?

## DESPERADOS

The floorboards were dark brown and creaked
and Mrs. Ellis who used to be Miss Jensen
brought forth a tiny, crazed marimba music
every time she moved her graceful legs between
the blackboard and the secret
border marking her turf from the province
of those eager front-row faces so firmly hated
by the rest of us, especially back-row laggards
like myself, who threw spit wads and giggled
snortingly and carved the word "tits" into our desks.

*Creeeek, snap, screeent,* "What is the capital
of North Dakota?"

"Tits!" we didn't say out loud.

*Hareeenk geeohhNEEP,* "How does one spell
'circumscribe'?"

"'Tee' 'Eye' 'Tee' 'Es'" we wrote in our all but
empty notebooks, leering and goosey with
the lusciousness of crime.

One day Mrs. Ellis, who was nearly too
beautiful to live, lifted her gaze
into our nether world of guaranteed failure
and probable arrest
and gave us all the tired pity she possessed.

The look went on and on.
The floorboards made no sound.
"Tits?" one of us wrote, experimentally

just as our faces flared with the shameful
knowledge that we would love Mrs. Ellis
all our ruined lives.

## THE "PRESIDENT" SPEAKS OUT ON THE ISSUES, 2006


It's Sunday and the President has finished his milk.
"Let out more line!" he hollers. A screen door bangs.

It is another day and the President has three shoes.
He thinks the closet is like his mother, hiding in plain sight.

The President feeds on charred animals, chewing their little ears.
It's Tuesday twice in a row in the unemployment line.

"I'm the President," says the President.
"I'll break every mirror in the garsh*darn* place."

It is a time of trials and the President is selling soap.
Lie soap. Carefully he washes out his mouth.

"War is our only road to peace," says the President
to his necktie and gloves. The wind smells of oily birds.

"Murderers should be excruciated," he tells his dog,
Spot, "So we can sleep safely on our boats."

It is Thursday again and the President completes his favorite
Norman Rockwell puzzle on national television.

"See what can be done if we work together," says the President
who evaporates below the waist and discusses the beauty of stumps.

"This is a great day, eh Spot?" "Yes," says Spot, "we all love you
for that." Then the third shoe begins to drop.

## MARSH

*—for Ray Amorosi*

Friend, I hear in your letters
a fine whiteness. Something like
a window sighing
for the plaited sleeve so
momentary now one might think
all companions folded
like doves in the apple grove.
Surely, all night absence burns
coolly described and wanting
just as all day the giant whispers
to his rings and I want to say so
much. Yet
we are the sky and the flight
of something like the arrow's hunger.
Are those lamps we hold as we dream
again of rain's bright shingle
dancing? Is it true
lives leave us like sparrows?
I am master only of these
questions and their branches
and I think you are so near
the stone in me floats and gives itself
a name to place in your pocket as you walk
beside the sea.
Do we deserve ourselves, I wonder.
Wind in the marsh grass, frost on the nest
of a crow, the loneliness of hills, everything
bewilders and blesses us.

## CIRCLES IN THE SHELL OF THE EAR


Everything I say I say everything
twice
everything twice,
though I'm a liar.  Most matters
mean so little to me, nothing
like the apples in my yard
though I have no yard.  Quiet plunder
goes on in the great malls.
Chickens are forgotten are forgotten.
There I go again.  I wish I had fingers
inside me to stroke and rinse the past.
The apple past.  And streetcars.  And holding
someone dear as a meadow, fog breathing above
in sunlight.  In sunlight breathing open
the door again to say again
be calm, this oblivion starts in you.  In you
this oblivion starts
and comes like apples I wouldn't lie.
All this I say will be again
forgotten again reborn again
forgotten.  In spite of which,
as every mercy is the soul
of mercy, one star winks
and listens and the rivers listen
in the great great night
out-of-into which we ourselves sail
ourselves, boats at last we can't explain
love in the face of love
in the face of God
's oblivious meadow, the soul
of mercy. I think I'll lie down I think I'll lie by
the lake of candles small in the vast

black of light inhaling light, breathing
our becoming again as I say
and feel again mercy's ex-
quisite sunlight candle
circling my ear and oblivion hearing
this mercy this boat
in my ear again setting out again
with an apple an apple
an oar.

## THE NEW CREATION

I slept on
while the world got up and showered,
made coffee, swore under its breath
at the headlines, and slouched off toward the bus.
Where was I, face
calm and red and unknowing
against the pea-green pillow?
I was simply elsewhere, maybe
wearing the silver spurs and purple hat
of a hero. Maybe riding hell bent
on a horse named Laddie or Target or Star.
Maybe the horse was red like the moon
dipped in rust
and while I rode him I turned red
in that glow. Maybe I was wheeling slowly
in deep space, a lone seed
searching for the womb that could bring forth
again the earth, our only home, refreshed
and secret, beginning again, dreamless
and possible, almost awake.

## UNACCOUNTABLE

The blue wolf was lonely, everyone said,
shaking with a palsy of commiseration
and secret joy. Surely,
we thought, surely color enacts both taxonomic
and temperamental distinction
so that it must be seen again
that Nature has her reasons.
Think of the crows, after all, the unmarked slate
of them so clearly a malignity, a strut
and want of civil flavorings, a sprinkling of original
dark chopped into squawking shatters by a fiend.
And so, we said, the blue wolf could know nothing
but the hollow night time of its solitude
where distant voices spent themselves in howling
and hungers of all kinds ran in packs.
It had for compensation only the blue stuff
of which it was made, and which we recognized,
though our fear and loneliness were greater
and though neither Nature nor Reason
accounts for this.

## SOMETHING BORROWED

Again I allow myself to see her,
twenty-eight now, maybe
getting married, clinging happily to me
as we move toward the minister or rabbi
or whatever
and the smiling bridegroom
whom I hate
only a little and whom I anyway imagine

has no sense
at all of what he's in for.

Sunlight is bolting down through the high
windows. Up among the roof beams
a trapped sparrow flutters and sings
as I hand her over, vowing silently never to tell
that she died eight years ago, leaving us all
in the suddenly empty church, the bird
like something flown out of us and circling
as this dream begins again.

## "I HAVE WASTED MY LIFE"
### —*James Wright*

Sun through pinkish green of the hanging
fuchsia. Two cats on the porch and a squirrel
high in the sycamore giving them hell.

I hope I haven't wasted it.

Often I've been in such hurry, burning
time like a draft card and staggered
by the pleasure of it. But there are so many

millions of us, who could say it matters

what one life burns or contains? Is it unforgivable
to say, "No one?" I'm thankful for the breeze
that does not answer

and for the cats that do not care.

I'm thankful for my children, even the one
who perished, and thankful for grief, its humane
and small respite.

Alone, I nudge my way upstream among others

of my kind. The rivers and oceans abound
with our loneliness, our dappled shadows.
I could weep right now for the mystery and ache

of days like this one, passing, almost

past before I touch or feel it
touch me like a memory that might belong
to a stranger I used to know, someone growing

into my body as I sleep.

## JULY

I open the door and there
is the lovely pointillism of the stars
and that coolness that consoles the roofs and streets
that have lain all day, helpless
in the flames of high summer.

A few others are out walking. I can see
far off, once in a while, the swinging
arms, flashes of lamplight
on clothing as they turn aside or go straight on
into the common mysteries of lives.

Just down the block a saxophone
smokes through a window with the news: "We're closer
than language lets us know."

I used to walk these streets with my first girl
after Doris Day movies at the Oregon Theater,
now a porno shop. I remember the crisp winter
rain and the smell of her coat
as I held her and marveled there was no word
for touching the damp face of a girl
leaned up to kiss me
under a blown streetlamp in the dark.

# MERCY

When she died, I reached through ragged fleece of the rain
for mercy, flailed
among nail box helplessness of the others and beside the wreck of
     ploughed light
with its crows.
All the next winter, ice clotted the blind roads and everyone
walked in halos
of their own frigid steam and the world was terrible and white
and I thought God
would surely speak, somehow save at least something from the cold
claw of that time.
But it was not His mercy, necessarily, I wanted. After all, in the very
     flowering
of her life
He had let her die. In truth, it was *any* brand of mercy
I desired,
any thin tungsten shell of starlight hope in the dark house
of those days,
any half-dead angel with one gift left to give.

Mercy had used to know me all the time. For no reason
whatever, seemingly,
beneath its gaze all the broken rocklike puzzlement of living
turned to fire-blue jade
and sky. I guess I thought *I* was a god, or something
extraordinary,
anyway, something blessed in spite of itself. But when she died
I just sat down
in that dust we come to, in the end. Just sat down, merciless
heap of sticks.

When mercy finally woke, it must have been a little dazed and wondering
to find such dark
crowding its shoulders and me like a nickel's worth of glass
asking, wrongly, for death

to be undone. I didn't care. I said these are my bones, all I have for an
        offering. Just
give back her life. Take mine.
And mercy took hold my hand, so I could turn and face the world and
        say this,
but that was all.

## VISITATION

Some of them came from the water
and some from green lobes and shingles
of their lanternlike machine. I thought
surely they were angels.
A small one with great saucer eyes
handed me an axe
in the shine of which
I saw the folly of my life, all
the wrecked harbors and rain, played
backward on an endless loop.
One of the creatures, their king, I think,
twelve feet tall and glistening like wet steel,
held out to me eighty-six roses,
calm spiders spelling out my name
on the stems. A great suddenness of noise
and whirling blackness came over us then
and the room was empty.
I could hear birds discussing the nature of light.
The door stood open.
I walked out into a field of scorched blades,
bent as though kneeling, praying for my soul.

## LOVE CALLS US TO THE THINGS
## OF THE OTHER WORLD

The wooden angel I gave my father years ago
looks down at me, holding its bright tin star.

Blond and smiling, she probably doesn't know he's dead
so I've gathered around her other mementos

to make sure she gets the message
or that I do.

On that same shelf is the church-shaped music box
I gave my mother on that same Christmas.

She's dead now, too, and I'm listening
to the ball game on the radio

and to a whole glee club of crickets
because it's late summer now in these parts.

One of my children has also gone over
into death, and some few of my old friends, though

I can tell they are near
in the fragrant and musical dark.

They care nothing for the outcome of the game, only
that it be part of the eternity

we have.
They may tell this to the crickets

by way of gentle teasing I think
I almost hear. Now and then

they look up at Cygnus breasting the great black shorelessness
of sky and I can feel

the purity of their lonely happiness creep up my arms
and the wooden angel winks at me.

# THE MYSTERIOUS COURTESY OF FONDNESS

What could it mean, this room, a piece
of time
so much like others and so much
its own
disheveled particularity in the life born
to me or given
or treed like an animal climbing away from fear?
Small, square, and hopeless, full
of light
for the sake of its windows, toppling and awry
with books, images and imaginary
doors, this room
accepts itself wearily, one old friend annoyed
by another but adjusting the curtain, proffering
the favorite chair because what else
is there now but the mysterious
courtesy of fondness?
I have been everywhere, flying this room
as though it were Spinoza's *scientia intuitiva*
or an arrow shot blindly toward the wandering
soul. And now
here we are
together, whole, and not very sad.
Outside is snowy wind and a life of glass
breathing in its winter den.
The room and I
make ever so small a bow
to what is other
and wish good days and nights, for all of that,
and all of us, camped on the lonely plain.

FROM

**THE CRIME OF LUCK**

(1976)

&

**WHY SHOULDN'T I**

(1977)

## THE WU GENERAL WRITES FROM FAR AWAY

My dear friend,
        it is snowing
in the house of my body, and beyond tarnishing
childhood
song, below the red
black earth our grandfathers loved.
        What shall I say of this summer
in which it is snowing
so often? I have no voice to describe
the delicacy of grasses, the scarlet horns
of new birds crying *feed feed*.
Every swayed limb stops the world
freshly. Every doe
browsing in sunlight beyond the meadow of tents
is a woman
releasing her braid on plain white silks.
        But it is going, it is all
going again through glass lips
of the hour. Soon cold will step from hiding,
the bears stagger comically to sleep, poor
beggars die out the crime of luck. Even now
courtesans lean to practiced grace
alone, shamed
as brushes draw youth on.
        Where shall we find hope
that cruelty is a passing accident, balance
the true gauge?
        I long to speak again kindly
with the thin dead
blossoms
who followed me here. I want to caress

the rose of peace before it empties, to abandon
storms over the ancestors of bodiless order.
    Tell me you have found it, the drowned
key, the footprint waking peacocks
at the last minute
which stops. You who followed the absent fortune
of pilgrims, come back to your friend
rooted here, sealed
in harm's garden of jars. Tell all
before snow retakes the road
to feeling,
this foreign ground.

## DEAR MRS. TERRY

Johnson said, "Yes sir, Mr. Carney,
right away, sir, aye aye," in his sleep.
The ship droned in the lead-hot
Gulf into which Cadet Pilot Terry shot
his plane, the impact of the catapult
socking him forward, his gear
snagging the stick. "I don't *know*, Captain,
he cleared the flight deck and went down
like a goose, sir." Fifty fathoms. Enough
oxygen for half an hour.

Locked in the chill black with his prayers,
wondering could divers find him so far
down, so cold, dark? No time to sing
into the squawker. Just that rush
of shimmered blue, the steely shadow
and the jolt as 41,000 tons steamed over
the closed seam that had allowed him
in, then darkening stripes of aqua through
the thick way down.

Black scotch broom pods snapped.
An old Chevy rolled past four years
of NROTC, sacrificed summers, haircuts,
harassment from fellow students: all
for this? Thirty minutes in a slow-filling
memory of light?

\*    \*    \*    \*

Water lapped. The whale boat came back full
of exhausted divers, sun scratching

the stanchions, the useless Day-Glo life preservers.
And Johnson slept, book
over his face, the writing of that next-of-kin letter
making a wide slow approach through the dead
chain of command.

## THE BELL MAKER

The stable glowed. Demon, the forge wanted
a crown—
silver clabbered copper, gold, antimony.

Years he bent and hammered. The perfect *Ave*
(he could hear it!) trembled above the town.
In his brain no seed, no lark

tapped the wind. He heard instead a shaking loose
of ringing prayers ached up the spire at God.
He made bells. His wife forsook him. His children

married rust. He made bells, struck sleep
with a slow rich tongue. The barn lay down
to ruin. Poverty

overtook his shadow as he worked. Then
sickness. At the end he clutched the surgeon
anyway, said, "It's up

up over the last life." When he died they searched
the loft and there was nothing but air
beaten to shapes faith might have found, the residue

of ecstasy, wrecked
harps
and angels melted down.

## HYMN FOR HIS HANDS

My grandfather had such long hands
they had to bury him
extra deep. Even now he keeps pulling
new sky above him, not from anger or the cold
will to escape, but from delight in change
wrought by his exquisite fingers.
Under my dream of summer and ploughing
I can hear him work, joyous
in the atmospheres of death. He hums.
He speaks of nothing as he sifts the dazzling beaches,
the harps his perfect hands play
perfectly. I speak to him often, though
there's no sense in it, or of it, and the priceless
urn of my desire to weep openly for love of him
is wasted on the photo album, the old dress shoes
I was married in, and the lamp that wakes me
burning out. So I shape with my hands
what I have to say and pass it down.
It's this: you did it right, all of it, and lived through
death. I'm alive, you know, and the world
that took the farm is taking everything
without much fight. So go on with your symphony
or dance. We hear your hands at the rough edge playing
roots and sky, and we have our hope. Whatever death is
never sleeps as you do. Harvester
of bright thick peaches, stay
in your bloom, in what forgives us. The times up here . . .
the times are frightening weather. Cells collapse
around the thorn of God. In black wind we search
the sleep above you for its craft

of mercy. And your hands,
slender as clues, loosen stillness, the strange
light extra deep
in us.

# CHANCE

I shouted warning, cursed as the square teeth broke
that life and let the feathers spin a slow rain
through the rest of day and into the dark.
It only meant to make a low pass

> *Out of control, bullets slice through the crowd.*
> *The arrow falls precisely inaccurate*
> *on the wrong deer (another fawn claws its severed spine*
> *into the sumac brake).*

by the barn.
But, like a gate slamming, the mare lifted her head
above the slat fence and into the piercing chord of that
old suitor of a chance misstep, old red claw, weasel

> *Orders come. "Exercise maximum force*
> *ratio in sector 'B', unfriendly" and are misunderstood*
> *by Lt. Calley, by a prehensile nightmare of triggers and pins*
> *and flight.*

rattling the stargate of an infant's sleep.
What bird could have known a horse would bite
through the probable order in less time
than life takes

> *Smoke hangs 20 years above rice paddies*
> *abandoned by the birds. Terrified cornfields shrink.*
> *The next ice age uncoils its colder*
> *and colder dream.*

to fly away.

Yes, this is about a bird eaten by the brown mare. Sunlight flutes on the muddied feathers. Crows pick the small head clean.

## THE ROSE FIELDS

The perfection of climbing roses is we cannot finally
rearrange them. They like what they are: spillage
on the dense light of summer. Grandpa had a bunch
of them. I remember by the greenhouse their red

and ivy against the white trellis. They kept on
growing after all supports went neglected
down, after the old man died. They kept on
spreading their elegant wrists across the field

and the last apple roots of dying orchard. Now
violent red cups peer through queen anne's lace,
bluebell, wake robin, iris gone to seed.
What's left of the farm goes that way, back

toward meadow and meadow lark. Even pheasants
occasionally wander through again. They sit
for hours in weeds they almost recognize
from before the Danish immigrants sailed in

on their ploughs. But they stare hard at the roses.
We stare at the shattered barn. Rake grey.
Yesterday I noticed field mice nesting beneath the roofs
of woven thorn. It's safer there.

Cats and owls leave them be.
They know about brambles, how the overgrowing
and the falling down of seasons covers death
with hunger, tangled hands.

## FIGURE FISHING AT NIGHT

He or she who stands
hip-deep listening
hears one answer as the strange arm lifts
like a question mark, casts fire
into fire. White scars the watcher's knee.
The scene is Gilgamesh adrift
and sighting up the starway: "Why
are we here?"

Slowly caught it is the god
Jupiter amazed at heaven.
Thin shadow of stillness
it is St. Brendan alone in the bow
of his cold century, steering by Antares.

A familiar harp burns in the creel, in fogbound
bands of blood arching moonward
and falling back. Amber. The sea
is within us, molten
brain pan sifting salt and shell music
in the abandoned shanties of salt and shells.

The night fisher reels in. One silver blade
follows, moon and mother
weaving through the Pleistocene, hooked
to itself
as the fisher is hooked to us.

FROM

**THOUGH SILENCE: THE LING WEI TEXTS**

(1982)

# INTRODUCTION: A REVERIE

In a New England town where I used to live there is an exceptionally peaceful wood. A small, bright stream runs through it, lending a light song to the general contentment of the place. Once in a while I would sneak away from work and spend a meditative quarter-hour on a mulchy embankment overlooking that stream (which we called Mill River), right above the prettiest S-curve a river ever made.

Fall was a particularly engaging season because then the stream was a moving patchwork of sparkling reds, yellows, oranges, and various greens. I would sit and watch this raucous assortment negotiate the turns of the S, some of the leaves gliding over the surface like cups of light, some of them weaving smoothly underwater like the voices of seven-foot alpine horns.

In that quiet place on a fall day, as I sat listening to the things Mill River and the leaves were saying to each other, I met Ling Wei; or rather, we encountered one another—for he said nothing on that occasion. He just came out of a thicket below me, on the far side of the stream, and sat down on the bank, relaxed but intent on the beautiful water.

When he looked up and saw me sitting there above him, he was somewhat embarrassed because he knew that I had made him up. And I got a little shy myself then, seeing that he was only a step behind making me up, too. So we watched each other and the moving chorus of things. When I got up to leave, Ling Wei (as I immediately thought of him) got up too. He made a little broom-like bow and I tipped my hat and we walked off in opposite directions. I saw him again three times before the leaves were gone.

When winter stuck in the branches, I would walk miles in the dark hours, smoking cigars and saying complimentary things to the snow with my eyes. It was on one of these little journeys that Ling Wei first spoke. I remember quite clearly his words: "Isn't snow a moonlight caught in the skull?"

It was a rhetorical question, of course, and it was exactly right: everything looked just like the moon made me feel. I said, "Thank you." And Ling Wei replied, essentially, "Don't mention it." And I never did. In fact I never spoke a word to my strange friend after that; it seemed enough to listen to him muse and babble on in Chinese (with English subtitles), and later to record the poems which tell of Ling Wei's exile and of his long journey—more or less as told to me.

He's gone now, back into the trailing edge of the 14th century. And I am gone too, I guess. This little book, though, keeps on—like Mill River and the leaves—, a thing we make together.

## LING WEI IN EXILE

Above the Valley of Birds
I pass four white trees. I sprinkle
drops from my waterjar and bow
to let them see I too am of rain,
light, and air, though my roots
are torn up and walking.
Not that the ways
of the wanderer must
be bitter. But I, having offended
the powers, go heavy with dust
and the clarity of nameless souls.
For me shade beckons with its thick
fingers; and in the valley's glittering
stream girls bathe and sing especially
sweet. Below in the village
roofs open to me like lilies drifting
beyond reach.

## LING WEI IN HIS REFUGE, WATCHING

Longer each night she tarries
in her boat
east of the mountains. For this
she has been scolded often
by fishermen who say, "She
that pulls the tide pulls also fish."
String fish, cod, and golden carp
especially rise with the breath
of that bright one, it is said.
Though I am not a fish, I too
feel the moon's nets about me
rocking the shimmer of fin
and scale into my brush. Helpless
my blood bows to the nightflower
jewel of rapture, dragging songs
and prayers like gifts, tribute
from the deep.

## LING WEI ON THE NORTH-ROAD

### I

I have been nine miles tonight
with the moon and dim
shapes of mountains breathing
in the west. Fence stones
sing damply in sharp air. No travelers
pass as I consider urgent speech
of the furrows. They say we are grass
to come. They say no one has love enough
to teach the wind
its clear direction, the water
what it shall sweep away.

### II

I hear the vague rasp of hay carts
bound for Tsitsihar and the chill-bit
North. Over dead farms and bones
of goats they are sliding away
with the hours. The dance of passage
is mirrors and the two-thousand whippoorwills
two-thousand years scattered among leaves.
The cart lanterns sway
like heads of ancient sages deep in thought
until all trace of them vanishes
in the narrow pass. Someone
out walking long ago
imagined the glittering worm of them
ghostly. Now they are gone into all the shapes
they might ever be. As I remember the old
wine-lit Taoist, my kinsman, who loved the mist
of these moments, they slip
into his drum . . . or

into rows and rows of grain nodding
above a burial place
beside the road.

## II

Lightless and hard, the way
through root fields glows with a grace
of sleeping herds. I should ask them
who they are, who tends now the space
they dream of filling after the grey moon
sinks and turns the world new.
I should ask the rotting silage
does it believe, can it
believe the net of the gods
bringing all things like strange fish
to this clay?

## LING WEI PARABLE

I came to a low rock wall
upon which an old man, his robes
yellow and tattered, sat speaking
with a cricket and a bird.
"Where are you going?" asked the man.
"Ah, where indeed is anyone going?"
replied the bird, before I could
answer—for the question had plainly
been put to me. "North," I said, "still
further north." The cricket ruffled
its brilliant wings and sang
"The North! Surely your feet
are much too large to walk in comfort
over those cold fields. Why
do you not climb trees?"
I was tired from ceaseless journeying so
I scolded the old man: "Why do you sit
in company with creatures who
with strange questions abuse the weary
who pass on this hard road?"
He thought for a long time, stroking
the thin cloud of his beard.
"Because I cannot get out
from under the sky?" he said.

## LING WEI'S SMALL SONG
## FOR HIS HOME VALLEY


It was a snow
place. A sun place with fingers
and women gathered among jars.
The river of it was
like memory piercing stone
just before light lays
its pure syllable
at the mountain's top
and the first ox leans
from the grass. Lute notes
fell all night into the blue plum
of heaven.
And such crowing
in the morning yards!
Even the young men flew
up from their delicate red sleep.

# FOUR CRYSTAL WOMEN STEPPING OUT

**I**

Under the hill, bears wander
endless dandelions. In bright
black of moon
        a snowy owl!

**II**

Singing, I walk by
the frozen stream. "And what of
his troubles?" No winds
        speak.

**III**

Stars dot out their shining
stories. Ground-squirrels observe
thought roaming the land.
        "And what of his troubles?"

**IV**

Somewhere, in a northern city, who
tends the pale geranium,
her open robe creased
        with sleep.

## SAYINGS OF THE BOATMAN

The world is a double
mirror; two evils,
two goods. Neither interested
especially in the other. Hooked
to the passing seasons they play, each weaving
through the emptiness of each
like fish chasing their tails. Also
the world is within you, all else is the vast
cold socket of pure sleep. Expect no comfort
from it. Also the dyad
universe is absolute and effortless.
Pay it no mind. Also trouble your thoughts
in no way. Seek nothing
but the delight of water
chiming over stone. This is
the Tao, to be both mirror
and mirror—one
in the double world.

## LING WEI'S FIRST DAY IN THE CITY

A harbor fallen
darkly, the storm
surrounds Tsitsihar.
The streets are barren
and bright through
wet hair slanting
off cornices & shrines.
By the wall some huts
collapse and naked
children shiver
in yellow muck, rising,
tugging at their toes.
Inside the stone
door-arch of one condemned
State building, my fire
sputters and I have
not rice nor mallow.
Still, what is contentment?
Rain is a gift, astonishing
the grasses. Hunger
keeps thought lithe
as a spirit cat. And later
I will build up my little blaze
to warm the children.

# SMALL IMPRESSIONS LOST BEYOND THE NORTH

### I

Branches of the spruce
lift and wave stiff
grappling with wind
and rain. Out on the zinc
waters ducks bob as if anchored.
There is a lone green skiff
on the storm.

### II

Back in silver birch draping
gold skirts against the cliff,
a house clings to its lives.
Fiercely its eyes stab yellow
shafts through the resolving dark air.
Is there a face at one window. Is it
the face of a tongue longing to say this.

### III.

Somehow a unicorn or dragon
is adjusting the snake grass.
Artisans believe this
thoroughly as they bend over jade
and paint. But I refuse
to speculate. It is enough that blood
can be wild horses leaping the River Yi.

### IV

So many swans today blossomed
from that blue
window of my heart
that I thought I had changed

into an azalea bush!
Then I thought, perhaps I have
*always* been an azalea bush!

## V

Leaves, cavalries of color and despair,
seek the gutters. Already
courtyards seem painted
by careless but cheerful workmen.
It smites me, this luxuriant lonely dying.
I almost wish the leaves were money:
less beautiful, but reverently attended.

## VI

Sea mist fills the deep valleys
like sleep. Along the inland rivers
where they broaden out in sunlight
enormous rooks break from shore,
pieces of night cast suddenly
from the lemon trees.

## PARABLE OF THE FORTUNE TELLER

There was a woman in the village of Tong Kow whose powers of clairvoyance were famous throughout the region. Each morning, at the ninth hour, she appeared at market with her goods—grains and sweet vegetables of remarkable brightness. To put a question, one had only to purchase some of her wares, which most were happy to do. One day a monk of the Chen Masters happened to pass through this town during the market time. Having heard of the great seeress who might be found in the place, he inquired and was directed to the woman. Sitting erect, her goods spread before her on a goat skin, she looked squarely into the monk's eyes as he talked excitedly of her fame and of his fortune at finding her just then.

"Fortune has no part in anything," she said. "We are simply here." Then, she explained that he must buy of her wares to partake of her services. The young monk was distressed by this, for he had no money.

"Do not be troubled," said the woman, seeing his perplexity. "I shall give you this pepper, but you must then allow *me* to ask the question." Somewhat confused, the monk nevertheless agreed. When she had given him the pepper, the woman said, "I will die tomorrow; who will be my successor?"

"I will," said the monk, astonished at his own powers of perception.

The next morning the ninth hour found the woman in her accustomed place. The monk, having resumed his journey, was far away.

## THREE LEAF-THOUGHTS FOR KUAN

I

Brilliant Face: the cove of Lu
darkens and teal break
toward the nonexistent
moon. A singing comes
over the glass water
falling. O!
it is the leaves
our brethren-in-time! singing
the chant of slow fire.

II

Today I walked, swishing
gold ruined books
like a god in splendid shoes.
"How is Kuan?" asked the red
voices of squirrels.
And I did not know, having
no letter from that far
province. So I replied, "He
has in ample stores for winter.
Have you?" And they left me
to leaves and wandering
and orange falling thoughts
of you my friend.

III

Answer with your next word
old walker, which
of all leaves falls heaviest
into the palms of those
who come with open hands
to the edge of the year?

## WHAT LING WEI THINKS ABOUT WAR

Loons crash on the frozen pond
beside my hut.
At night I go out to them.
Writhing in broken wings
they seem scarcely to hear the poems
and meditations I recite
in my quietest voice. Soon their bills snap back,
one red foot clutches terribly
the starred air.
These strange destructions
sadden briefly the bare tulip trees
who must look on with me.
After proper silence we discuss it.
The trees say, "We wave our branches furiously
to warn them as they come down;
but, alas, their eyes see only one side
at a time and they are lost."
And I shrug and say, "Don't blame yourselves;
only tell me, what
can be done for the bruised ice?"

# WINTER SEQUENCE

**I**

The year contracts in cold and white
like a brittle leaf. Snow goose, snow leopard,
and silver fox rise up
from chill air near the ground
as if winter light had made them
visible for the first time.

**II**

Nothing moves on the path
except the path
and moonlight circling dark sticks.
I came this way for reasons
of wood and brightness. On such a night
my flute is two stars
trapped in an ice-covered cistern.

**III**

Houses cramp around what heat
they have. This bitter blood
in the air confronts them
like axe-thought and flame.
It is battle to the death! Stay
out! stay out! cry the houses,
slamming their cloaks.

## DEVIL-MERE

There is a flat stark water
where swans choke
on their reflections, and the bear
will not stoop to drink.

Once in the mountains I saw it,
slicked with ice and a strong
moon: a story forced like wind
through glittered jaws of the deer skull.

From pine groves it bade me
come forth, scattering
my arrows. "Drink
of the blessedness that burns,"
it said. And I went down
over the white years and did not,
almost, come back, singing
to my fire.

For when I bent to that
face, it was
history? and such a shining
in the frozen things
I had loved! Such a rare
eternity of voice! Such brimming
emptiness. Such a deep
hard lake of time
and grey stones.

FROM

# SEA CHANGE

(1985)

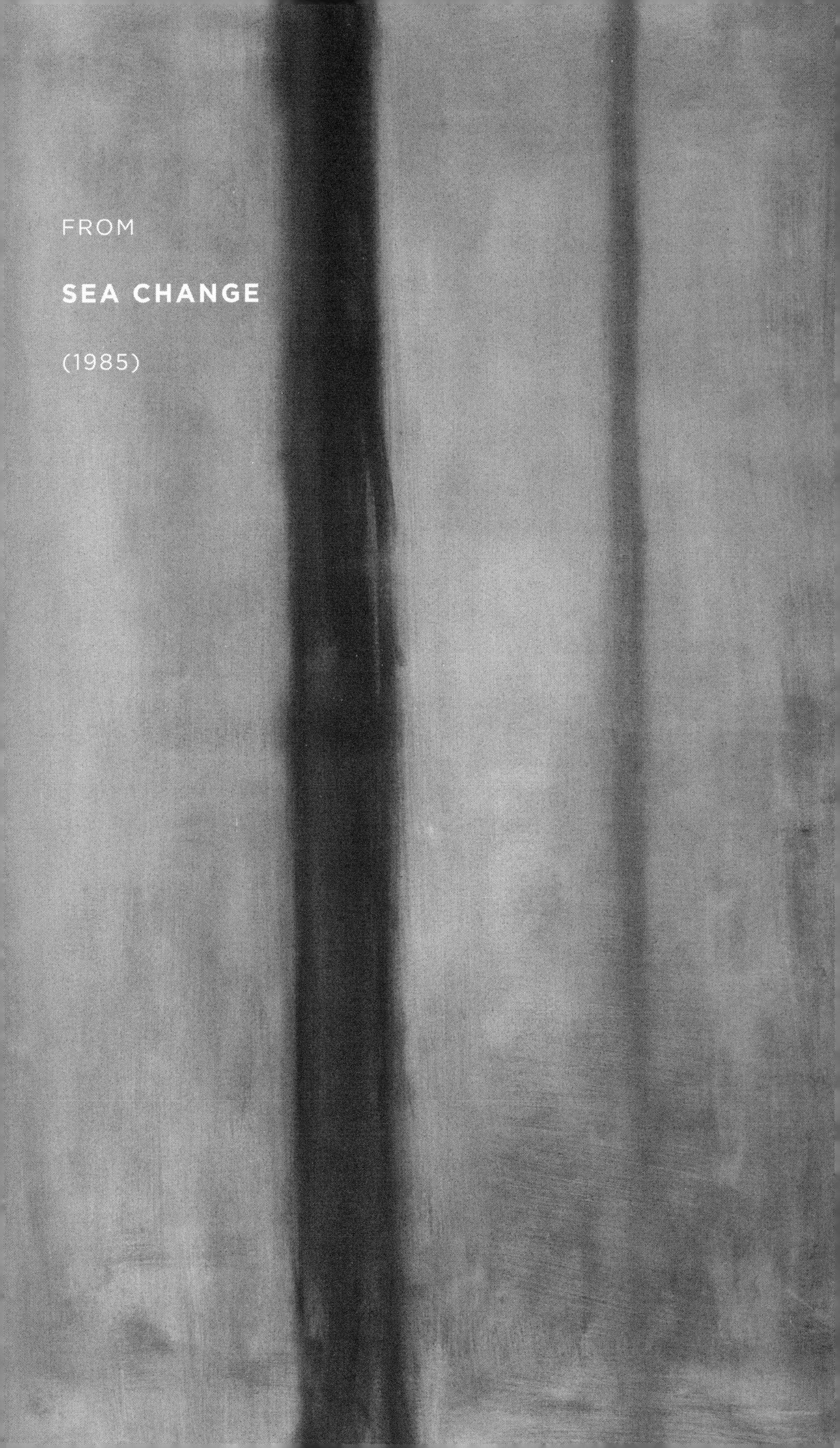

## ABOARD THE SAN JUAN FERRY

That we coast island to island
in our named lives
is nothing to bother earth's gleaming
blood. Above us, as the ferry swings
in toward shore, sea birds whirl
like bits of paper in the blue bowl
of the day. "We have come,"
we say. "We have made another
crossing, and the sea behind us
is entirely new."

## A REMINDER TO THE CURRENT PRESIDENT
*—for Lewis Cook, 1945–1969*

On an average afternoon men lay down
rifles, leaning into heat
from which a few will not rise
again. "It is because of shrapnel,"
we say. "It is because of hatred
and ageless dispute and love
of country, which we have learned."
Though the cleanly young seem deathless
as this language passes over them,
neither the *zip* nor the sound of the plane
nor the singing wakes them.

On an average afternoon
by the trimmed shores, pacing, waiting
for news, the loved ones
approach the exact moment
which will not decode: a projector runs
on and on in a dark theater
and the doors are locked. A drum roll
circles the drill field. Carbines
sound once, twice, and again. Who
will cast dirt down into the cool rest
of itself? Why does the film go on
showing and showing these few gathered
in sunlight around a space so empty
only the earth can fill it?

Questions. We are advised to let them ride.
We are advised that life continues.
That, on an average afternoon, the mother
will be given medals and a speech.
That all of this will be long ago,
like an unused wisdom.

"God's flag is our flag," it says
in the handbooks. "Therefore, be comforted
and clean of conscience: these deaths
are part of a plan." Meanwhile, the film
is rewinding; and the sound of a plane sails
the dimming heavens, far off, like a telegram
on its way.

## AT THE EQUINOX

**I**

It is after the rain
and before the rain
and the smell is a smell of soil
drinking and sighing.
Dogs play with the vacancy
of the vacant lot across the street.
Birds are dipping very fast
very suspiciously;
in the gun-blue air
all of them are black.

I can hear a tree nearby
beginning to hum out a little Mozart,
beginning to break the vows of silence
trees take, beginning (what the hell,
it's spring) to let go
of her impossible strength.

The new shower falls
or rises from the ground
and a short avalanche of birdsong,
like a cheer, rushes from all directions
to nest in the branches
of the non-conformist.

**II**

Now day is nearly gone.
My white cat is the only cat
in sight. He crosses the road
to leave his scent on some bus tires.

Softly he calls to one of his brotherhood
hidden in the darkness. Then
he comes back
and watches the white rose
draw night slowly down
around its shoulders.

## FLIGHTS THE WIRE BIRD WATCHES
*—for Carlos*

Low hills white, soft
humps in the waning day.
I am bound out
past saloons, whitewashed
former gas stations selling tacos,
fifteen farming equipment companies:
ragged edge of a county seat in the West.


Brown rouge clings
to the valley. Bright broken fists
of the Cascades lurch up
from cloud-choked distances.
A wire bird in a cornfield
breaks thinly into song.
What I wanted was not here.
Where I'm going the wire bird knows.
See, how joyous his singing,
how clear, among the crows.

# IN GREY WATER: THE DAY

### I

Slack tide before dawn.
The rental boats
have just finished singing.
A blue heron slivers, exact
glass at the grey edge
of grey water. Light aches
like a lover deep in the reeds,
in the pit of the willow shaking
with dark. Mussels, the violin
bones of flounder, all dead
given up by the nightly sea
arch in a tuning of instruments.
Memory and sun collide in the lungs
of stones and mud, breathing
the alchemical father, burning the skin
from his dream. The heron gives
his wing to the first shaft
of knowledge suddenly torching
its own face. For an instant,
which is the sea, and which
the bitter shore? Then morning lifts
its flat conch wail.

### II

On thick glass the grebes
and sawbills move
like light finally
    broken
through waves of rain. I
    bend to that
mirror the starved

face of a reed. I ask, my
lips barely moving, for depth
    and power
and a sure, unselfish mind.
Clouds appear, sliding
like ghost-riders
into the southeast. The water
shakes from its trance,
    dissolving
the lives held there
and the supplications
which rise and are carried off
by the kingfisher
who has mistaken them
for the shimmer
of living things.

III

Barnacles and mussels
seem the heart
of the matter: there are so many
destroyed white faces clinking
and clinging to stones.
And they have voices like sticks
    snapping. All day
they argue cosmologies, relentless
as the salt which scrapes them
clean. It cannot be *the stars*
*are a wheel of winking*
    *pearl; all lands planets*
*in a universe of sea.* It cannot
be *God is a heron*
*from the far side of the cove.*
    Hours deepen
toward the minds of roses

far inland. Tide collects
for the long climb back
up the seawall, over moonwhite
        collars
of the dead. Over the heart
of the matter.

## IV

Over water the twinkling
half-star windows of my country
come. Broken fences and battered
doors go with them. Voices
        of bruised
lives are nearly still. We have
        been surprised
by quiet and the warm rippling spears
of light on water, water on the face
of the mind. Discouragements
do not matter. Acrimony
        lies idle
licking its paws. What we know
is night and dark drifting with teal
far out in splashes of moon
and shadow. Tonight I am
        praying
again. I am praying the torn tongues
of Earth, the carborundum lament
of industrial sedge. What we keep
is what we allow no breaking of.
Membranous and steady, like wind
moving in the darkening neighborhoods,
we seek the far shore. And window light
breaks from us
like the sound of oars.

## KEEPING WATCH UNDER A LAMP POST
## IN THE DEEP WOOD I EXPERIENCE
## THE CARESS OF ANOTHER WORLD


So you have come at last,
my portion, circle
of light on the edge of the hill
of dark. I thought
you would be longer, narrowing down
from sun to the pool of yourself
hung above me in the beeches.
                          I thought
I would look out from your hand into stillness
puzzling the snow like footprints of a god.
But here you are, iced cyclamen
shuddering with wind. No women
follow you through the ruin of trees,
no friends at all heft axes over the fields
ritually asleep. It's just two
                of us
trying to stay warm,
trying to say old roots twine in the deep
earth places, brother,
sister, keeper of what lasts
from one hill to the next.
We know it isn't love
buys this small space against the owls
                          of blood
speaking their nameless question.
Still, midnight finds us kissing
just the same. Unknown lover
this kingdom of sticks
my life

burns like a black barn yearning for a heart.
The face of you worshipping no cup or stone
is not a fool's craving.
   All right,
I mind my tongue
and keep my absent windows clear of God,
waiting like all desolate stars
for the light that never comes from you,
for the novas of the grass.

## LIBERTY & TEN YEARS OF RETURN

*—for the veterans*

### I

In the singed breath of London
we were lost
and aching sailors burnt by ships.
Disgusted, lonely, broke we four
buddies went adrift, sealed
casks of withered lust. Above the dim
lamps our President kept saying, "No.
We love a rigid chaos. Get laid
if you like, but nobody leaves."

### II

A few cops passed like blue
trees moving. A taxi splashed dark
on our dark American frowns.
Hours we spoke of the trains, chanting,
mythical; of penalties
for missing muster, ship's movement,
the long glide home. At last, shivering
we stared down years of open windows
till the third-class cars pulled out
for Portsmouth in the teeth of dawn.

### III

None of us expected this
arrival, the band strewn dead
on an empty pier, the fleet crusted
and opening like a bowl of dazed peonies
to the chalk sky. Now
we see: ours is an absent life, no healing.

Sent over the great sea
a decade has returned us with no riches,
no message, and no home waiting
or wanting us here.

## PAID IN FULL

A man opens his mouth to spit or speak rapidly.
Thousands of erasers tumble out.
They are the silence keeping ahead of him, the lack
of a future, the history he will not look back on
that will not look back on him.
                            The erasers gather
lovingly around him, erasing first the mouth
then the nose, ears, and the rest of the face.
Leaving the eyes, tragic and wide, in a clear space
above the body.

Through the eyes the man watches
all the dear labor of him
erased, beginning with carefully chosen cigars
and personal accouterments.
                        The rug and walls
go quickly. The wife takes a long slow sob of hours.
The arsenic blue floating eyes widen and fill with blood.
The man's body disappears in a frenzy
                                of pink shavings. Now
only terrible eyes plead
                    in a windy field.

The man who is not
sees that all things are without him.
He sees the beauty of before he was,
                                or after.
He sees the erasers writing on the frosted glass
of Heaven: *All speech and all longing*
*to speak erases the self, to some degree.*
Now you are paid in full.

## RAMON'S LETTER

I broke the stone
I did not mean to break
the nightingale
caged preciously in the digress
moment of today's mail. Ramon,
this year was wet, last year cloudless
and dry—the inland gulls became beige
drifts of dust. I continue in my faith
that lilacs will sweeten me
if I eat enough of them.
Stubble and wind and a headlight
drunkeness keep me
a little sad. Also, I thicken, like a tree,
roots bursting in to the cistern
on a nondescript afternoon in March.
You write no letters, but I get news
of you; how you sit
piquant, tilted back with a beer
and a garnet arrow which is called
*virgin*. Feed it the broken nightingale,
why don't you, the shards of rock.
Be sure the smoky blood left over
makes someone weep for that face
of yours, catching the brick
Auld Lang Syne of love
delivered for a fee.

# SEASCAPE

*Out on the Pacific, in that green*
*air studded with sharks,*
*a veil is blowing over the ghost ships*
*of Miguel Ortiz. What gold or love*
*or language in them, the dolphins know.*

\*

On your raft, be quiet
about the lack of food and the way
current guides your death
with huge paws. If you could catch
a dolphin, it would only be a singer,
dancer in the heavy wind
like you. If you could call out like an unmuzzled star
to the great whale within you dreaming
of another age, you would lie to him
always. This is fate, voice awash in the chest
wound of the sea. Listen
at your peril, but listen if you can.
*Lost* is just a word, like *cloud*,
like *homeward* and *chain*. It isn't yours,
drifting planet, anymore. Nothing itself
swims past the reefed dictionaries in all the lands.
So the planks divide
and a salt blood covers you in life
as you go down? Rescue is only wind at play
on the long prairies of water.
Your choice is to believe it and drown,
or to drown, simply.

## THE VOYAGE

An obsidian boat vibrates
in the heart of a cloud
above Martinique. The crew,
in chains, moves with blue insistence
toward the idea of water.
The sky is solid waves
of rock and wind
ignites the only map.
Now and then something alive
is thrown overboard. "No one
asked you to come along,"
the Captain, horrible gob of dissolutions,
says, pouring another glass
of fire. "Well, you're in for it
if you think this is bad?" Claws
come out of the deck
and deal with the complainers.
It is a huge enterprise, by all accounts,
revolutionary. They are going to discover
the Islands of Commerce, those bland
and equitable kingdoms
where success is breathable, not a lie
at all. The ship yaws, taking on lava
and screams. "Oh they don't
make a bloody crew like they used,"
the Captain observes, boiling hideously.
The boat, *Lucky Forever*, steams
into a treatise on late 20th-century
starvation, where it capsizes. The Captain,
secretly sure all along that the voyage
has been madness, says, "Christ!
We should have stayed in Hell."

## THE PITCHER'S PRIDE

At sixteen I wanted only
the hard laced scars
of dead horse
blurring from my fingers
as the batter winced
and rode forward
into failure. All dreaming
was a pistol shot,
the ball exploding
in the catcher's glove,
the ump's right arm flying
up, recording the kill.
On my little tower
of earth I was close
enough to God:
I could see my sin
dissolving in the thunderclaps
of His applause. *Atta way*
*to fire, my son.*
When the arm went
years later
in rainy McMinnville
I had prayed forgive
please thy humble servant
his power to mow 'em down
to bleached fear and the dull
lives calling slowly in
across the trimmed outfield
turned brown.
I paid for that
by wanting,
every day always

through the ice packs
and cortisone
and my own brown grass, wanting
forever
one more game.

## THE DEATH OF GIOVINE
*—for Lew Giovine (1944–1981)*

Giovine went out among the darkling
up-sprayed winter trees, when the snow came
soft through an eternity of sky
as though the Earth were calling back
fragments of its angels
who had gone off somewhere and stopped singing.

Giovine went out among a deepening bright
reflection and had no fear at all.
Smoking and walking and losing his way,
he yet thought, "This is a fine grove, and this.
See, though I am lost, the blessings rise up
around me." Thus he spoke, old Giovine,
loveliest of word makers, good king of stones
who carried no stones, who walked
for the love of walking
when he could have flown.

And then he sat down to rest
under the resting hemlocks, the cold
hemlocks that later called and called
to wake Giovine who had gone off—like the angels—
walking and singing in the other world
while his body sat as though thinking
of good friends and wine and a morning
fairer than this one, fairer than any
morning that has ever been.

FROM

**SWEET AFTON**

(1991)

SWEET AFTON, Pennsylvania, Oct. 1, 1937. The town of Sweet Afton, Pennsylvania, disappeared under millions of tons of water today. While some 600 of the town's 1,438 residents looked on, the lake formed by the newly erected Bishop Dam on the Afton River—a tributary of the upper Allegheny—closed over the spire of Sweet Afton Congregational Church, the tallest structure in the town, ending weeks of amazed, angry, and, at the last, silent waiting.

Today's events put an official end to the community's six-year struggle with Ward-Whitson Power and federal agencies to preserve its existence. Throughout the numerous meetings, hearings, and court actions citizens argued their right to reside in their chosen surroundings. A final appeal was denied in January by the Third Federal Circuit Court.

Refusing Ward-Whitson's repeated offers to move substantial portions of Sweet Afton to higher ground, to the very last, residents were nearly unanimous in their determination to halt construction of the Bishop project.

Workers were continually harassed by small-scale sabotage and open derision from onlookers during the three-and-one-half years of actual construction. Said one worker, who declined to be named, "We began to wonder, after awhile, if what we were doing was right. I know I'd be unhappy if the government decided to do this to my town."

Cloudia Brown, a longtime resident of Sweet Afton, reported much the same and added, "I think this whole affair has been a scandalous breach of democratic values and process. If I weren't so old, I would leave this country, as some are planning to do, I understand. For the most part, though, I suppose we'll just take our compensation cheques and drift away. It is unspeakably sad."

The dam is expected to meet the water needs of the rapidly expanding Pittsburgh metropolitan area until at least the end of the century. However, that the water was designated exclusively for Pittsburgh, 100 miles south of the dam, was another sore point among district farmers and other local residents who felt that the area should reap at least a portion of the benefit for which an entire town was to be sacrificed.

Sweet Afton was founded in 1728 by Elias Nicholsen and his brothers, descendants of whom were still among the town's leading citizens at the point of its forced disincorporation four months ago. Principal products of the community were fine lace and canned fruit, both industries controlled by the Nicholsen family.

Outside Pennsylvania, Sweet Afton was best known as the birthplace and residence of Eldon Achilles Clay, noted naturalist, and the pastoral painter Plato Hall—whose painting "Lovers in the Dark" hangs in the National Gallery. Both men, who came to prominence at the end of the first decade of the century, are still living; but like all who once inhabited this quiet rural town, their present whereabouts is unknown.

## OLD NICHOLSEN HIMSELF

For commerce there was what we have
today: shoes, lace, saw blades and canned fruit
of the quince. One Errat Myke made knickers
and cheap linen wares. The poor were so poor
that everybody helped them
twice a year, and after funerals.

For building we had pine drug out of the wild north
where the few remaining savages did their dancing
it was said. The whole town was wood, even
the jail where Eustice Springham was the drunken
nightly guest for thirty years. "Clean living" kept him
with us far too long was everybody's joke
until the fire of '14 sent Eustice up in pickled smoke
to meet the Head Man. Reverend Swan said

he could just hear the old boy holler for the Lord
to "set 'em up!"

Enough. You know by now our history
is one man at a time
looking for sweet life's milk in a rotting linden tree.
Some found it, incredibly enough, though not me.
God curses those who think they are too good
for the hunt. What I found is what I knew
at once, the town is your only heart,
and death's coming.

# PALE RACHEL'S ANCIENT POINT OF VIEW

Parma the scent of the age, and Lillie
Langtry's sultry face. What a man asked of his horse:
to bear gentility at window level
so that any could see it who would.
Papier poudre like fine snow
astonished the moonlit nose of every lady, redolent
in taffetas (rose-pink and mauve—the sweetpea shades)
that rustled as they walked.

Night after night the air filled up with trilliums
and the great manse swayed. There were
chestnut trees, then, and the smell of lime leaves
captured by manure. And all night after night
the sound of hoofs and carriage wheels.
Rouge, my sweet, was what we wore
in praise of light. And black to praise death,
though we didn't know it. Just as the menials

wore red to celebrate what they could have done to us
but didn't know it. Long golden afternoons, too—
I have seen them; so many, who could count?
All outward mask. There was poison in those cups of tea
that should have flattened Rome to think about.
All those feathers, too, were not a songbird's plumage; no two
alike, but all identical—like jealousy, my sweet
dead sisters and friends, like every summer evening promenade
lined up cradle to grave. "And back," you would like to hear
me say. Instead I tell you, "So would I," and pass on that
tempting rhyme. It can go with the rest of us
to the Devil, or to the world that nearly was.

## MASTER RONALD WESTMAN,
## EXCLUDED FROM THE TEA


Oh these ladies in the garden, their big
hats like clouds uncertainly adrift
in the moving daylight; parasols
slow tops upside down
above the eruptions of lace
everyone is wearing.

My aunt makes me hide
in the corner room where I go over
and over a bit of Aeschylus:

*Alas, Helen, wild heart*
*for the multitudes, for the thousand lives*
*you killed under Troy's shadow,*
*you alone, to shine in man's memory*
*as blood flower never to be washed out;*
*surely a demon then*
*of death walked in the house, men's agony*

Sure, domestic, the plot grinds on
and I reread reread these lines
and peer over the sill at wicker
and silk and flowered china
and the cool mysterious women
who coax the garden into early bloom.

Oh those hot
scones as they pass the lips!
So this is agony; my member
like a rail as I behold them
leaning and laughing and lifting their cups

so far from me
who can read Greek and French
and play a cello like the grown man
grown into my sinful hand.
Ah, the seedcake!
So this is Helen.

## CLOUDIA'S ANGEL

To the angel on the wall
at the foot of my bed I give
one kiss.
That is what I am allowed
to give suitors
upon the occasion of rejecting them.
"It will be a consolation, the poor dears,"
old Nanny says. Though
I believe it makes them want
a deeper taste of this
satin lily, painstakingly pleated and composed:
myself. "I don't want them," I say, slowly
bringing my lips back
from the smooth plaster face
my uncle painted years ago, a charm
to make me sleep. Blue,
white and gold, it is nothing of the world
reaching out for an embrace. Its wings
curled to catch air, hold perfectly
still the long straight body
that is a woman's when I dare
to think on it. It has never bent
low over the bed
to touch or whisper in my dreaming ear,
"desire, Cloudia . . . is what
you're made for."
But in the careful rooms
and gardens of the town, something
like that comes to me
over the soft clicking of heel
against heel, lies soft on the edge
of my cup that rises and rises

until I see, as on a plaster wall reflected,
my own distant face
asking the angel, "Are you cold there
in that pure place?"

## ELDON CLAY AND THE REVEREND'S WIFE

We will meet by the river
or the breath of it.
Where the sawgrass parts
for a small quilting of moss
we will disrobe and sway
into one another like the shadows
of two trees. What we will learn
is the depth of the body's ache,
that longing only grows more natural
and warm as we reach the blue edge
that holds us back from death.

This is not wisdom, but
walking home in the rich dark
I dream your arms flung up
around your husband's neck, holding
the smooth contentment of a single life.
This wretched heap of shattered glass,
my self, knows love a magic beast
bedazzled, perfectly at rest in the myth
that life is not what kills us.

So I dream you and remember and believe
in nothing. Let the town whisper
what it will: "The preacher's wife's
committed sin with Eldon Clay!"
The only measure is our morning
of wet white skin
among the reeds. For now, the straitened
single life has only platitudes to say.

# BLUESTOCKING

"You mustn't speak about mathematics,"
Mother said. "It discourages them."
Religion, Greek Literature, and the fate
of Democracy were likewise not approved
discourse. That left banter, gossip,
and trivial indecencies of the modern stage.
I was bad at it from the start: curtseying
on the wrong foot, calling Lionel Umbreidt
a fool because he thought *Antigone*
"a disease of cattle and other bovines."

*Mundus vult decipi.* It seemed
no man wished to earn the right to me.
They wanted me won in a game of dices,
the lucky man to spread me out admiringly
like a fan. They wanted just enough dancing
to get the job done, and "please, no rhymes,
Miss Emiline."
God, there was a pack of them
parading to our house, leaving their pretentious
cards in the music room.

*Satis verborum.* I walked over the hills
and gave young men no names at all.
Among patches of brown and green,
over low passes where you could look out
and see sweet lovely Earth for miles,
through meadows of doves heart and merrythorn
I went, carrying my books.

*Knowledge and freedom must one side of love . . . .*
As for the other, *amo ut invenio* and no shame

to any passion. And the one great love,
he never showed. And now I have one foot in a book,
the other ever deeper in the Earth it loved
to walk upon. The town is gone, poor
silly fools. I miss them
but the whole lot made me laugh.

# EDGAR CLOONY'S COURTSHIP OF MISS EMILINE

While the Viennese waltz washed over us,
a finger-tip and arms-length business, I kept
one constant aim: to touch, so slightly
she would never know, the pale pink velvet
cupped side of her breast. All longing
must have risen through my face,
for later, at the dark edge of garden
where couples walked murmuring in secret,
she took my hand and
slipped it
into her bodice (Christ!)
and said, "There, is that
what you wanted?"

Oh, how her laughter hunted me
as I ran.

## THE RUNAWAYS' STORY

The strap was never spared us,
nor a sharp cuff on the ear.
That was why we ran away
from the brick school face
of Mrs. Kyle one spring day
at noon. Life, along the lanes
and through the buttercups,
was one large lemon drop.
An old man on a milk cart
gave us each a dime
to "run along home;" but
we didn't do it. Elizabeth said
we should swear never to go back
till we had seen Pittsburgh.
In the same blue pinafores
we wore eternally to school,
we followed road ruts through
calico light like a set of orthodox
birds. No matter darkness came
caressing the trunks of the trees.
As the track slowly lifted into
evening, I confided to an owl
a blackening distress. "Scared"
Elizabeth said. And I could see
her white face
when everything else was dark.
I see it still, disappearing
as it did that night (blown out
like a candle in a windy shed)
never to be seen, on earth, again.
Nearly every night I dream
I am the one
who's waiting to come back.

## ELIZABETH'S STORY

There was a darkness I could bear,
then there was the unbearable swiftness of pit
that took me, soundless, down
to no light. "No more," I thought, "there'll be no
light anymore." Sarah's voice
reached for me as I fell, "Elizabeth, Elizabeth! Don't
*do* that *Lizzy* it's too dark. Elizabeth? Where
are you?"

The floor was a piney jolt, and no mistake.
The breath flew from me and the air
around me rang like winter bells. Then I died,
I think. Out of a hole of light above me
some angels came on long beautiful ropes.
And I was lifted up and there was broth and fiddle
music, and a great amount of dancing.
The language of them was so quick
and wonderful, I closed my mouth
till I should learn that speech. I did not ask
to see Pittsburgh or say my name or cry out for Sarah.
I thought myself dead, you see. So I went
with them in their moving houses
over a countryside so like Pennsylvania, I thought
there was a double world.

At fourteen they began to let me out
to men. Huge and boozy the railroad workers stood
in lines to mount me in the tiny spangled wagon
where I lived. I hated it
at first. But later I died again and the angels grew afraid
of curses I might work. And so they set me free
in a heaven so unlike Pennsylvania and so far

away, I'll never find the ladder out. And anyway,
the nuns here say Sweet Afton is no more. And I am old
and mad
and I have no blue pinafore.

## OLD LECHER ERRAT

She was standing under the chandelier, as I recall
it now, in full fig: something white and
about six pounds of beads—including a pearl choker.
Ah, such bosoms beaming up at God! And a fair

sassy jaw to tell you what she gave a damn
not for. Woman born to grace
and bed. I knew it from the start.
Unhinging the fixed ratchets of my slyest art,

I did assail her there at the ball
while the merry folk with serious faces
led quadrille upon quadrille to the swaying floor.
She would have none of it,

at first. "Sir,"
she said, "I do believe you've had your tongue
in dirty ink." And next, "Would you care for a lump
of coal?" By God, a smashing girl!

## PLATO HALL

Down Third Street and into the park
I wander with the first full summer
light each day. My paints and brushes
and my linen flats wake and come along—
though often they will not see
what I wish them to.

Sometimes, humming a tune, we ford
the river in loud shallow water
near Collier's mill. Then over meadows
with bright or tumbled barns
and sometimes workers bending
in the fresh hours before heat
dazzles the shocked grain. Mauve
and violet and green
among the blue and yellow I deploy
for wonder's sake. I work, at whiles
to the brink of dark
before I know the workers have gone home
and the fields are full
of solitude again. And then sometimes
I paint that too and wake
hungry, covered in dew, surrounded
by strange tiles
scattered by a sleeper as he danced.

Often lovers I have met here, or on the hill
swaying in alder groves,
and once by the river on a large flat stone.
Gold finch and morning glory make
the shades of their desires, light
on water their unknown, unspoken hope.

So quietly I paint them where they lie
or walk, they never guess my face
from reeds or branches.
And never would I
dishonor them. Like me the work stays
hidden in my small house in the town.
Let time accept it, possibly, or flames
or dust or rain. In this too
let the paintings be what they depict.

Oh, all the townsfolk I have seen
and taken to my brush for some sake
not my own. The few things I do sell
I sell for no great golden fee.
Most of my sad companions here will never know
the single object of the work
is joy.

# THE SPINSTER ANNIBEL COLLIER


Who wanted to grow up? *Wind*
*in the Willows* gave us girlhood hand in hand
with *Dream Days*, and several other paradigms
of one long day or season
that had no breasts—nor any reason
for them either. Romping on holiday
amongst the clumps of gorse by the shore
we wore not much, sometimes
nothing.
          Of course
that depended on the wind. If chimes
on the cottage porch rang too heartily, we understood:
flying sand marks the white meadows of girlish skin.
Marks, burns, and blemishes were not examples of the good
flowing through us because of what we were. Sin
was for farm girls from near Edwardville Wood,
where what we longed to speak of happened
ceaselessly, we heard.
          Where the dark goat turned
its eyes inward and beheld a light. The band
from Demon Town played there every night and burned
the arms of the twining holly trees. But we
were pure and meant by lineage to stay that way.
You would have seen us dreaming in the lee
of some dune, lifting up our hair, about to say,
"My, what if a pair of princes should surprise us
in all our absent lace?"
          Laughing,
perhaps we watched gulls on the blue mirror, lovely
like this one that will not now reflect a lovely face,
or dip into the grave for you my rose, my prince, my sister
only.

# THE GALLERY OF PLATO HALL

### 1 *Portrait of the Unnamed*

Which face is it
in the green grass and the wind?
The lover's face? The stone tablet face
of a god? Perhaps, knowing weather,
endurance, and the blossoms turned
to earth turned to blossom. Still
it is only a face, or that idea of face
weeping in us all
under the spell of winter—any kind
of winter, believe it, believe it
absolutely. But which face
is it?

It is the secret face of delight
in form burning the cool green grass,
striping the wind that shakes the willow leaves.
All we have given up, all we have
longed for or destroyed, circles this secret
face, which is so like the face we hold
in our hands, like the doctor holds
in his hands, amazed at this singular
thing which is emerging
again for the first and final time always
and instantly becomes the wind and the cool
bright green grass.

### 2 *Song for the Sweetgum Tree*

Oh the sweetgum tree, more full of joy
than lonely, keeps

beckoning my only winter song. A beauty among
all the wreck of beauty
hill by hill, she sways, holding
her exquisite declensions up to silver light
as though waiting for a god more kind than we
know or care
to know, as if grace breathed back
through grey arms of the loam.
The woodsman, whose glittering axe hews
stand on stand of tamarack, stops
at the sweetgum and cannot lift his blade
for wonder and for love, cannot cut
down ever this one that I am thinking of.

## 3 *Pastoral*

Hazelnuts drop on the country road.
In the ruts along both sides
goats wander like alien flowers, puzzled,
benign, in no hurry
to discover why they are here.
The leaves talk with the dry precision
of orange, one joke after another,
their speech the subtlest
clear gift of season. You must be still
to make it out. You must quit
the riot of your own deep tongue
screeching its one idea all day and on
into sleep. You must fall, like the hazelnuts, softly
back to earth and lie for the first time
as if you had returned
happily, absently
to nibble the pigweed.

**4**  *Geese by Yellow Hill*

Where dead limbs dip
down into voices of the crickets
undergoing their curious arrests,
and where only the melancholy
and the carefree ever find themselves
looking absently up into dusk,
where what the dreamer longs for
becomes strange and giddy
with the taste of its disasters;

a yellow hill steps suddenly
from a meadow where thousands
of geese wander
because, though there is danger, this
is where they always stop.
Some scouts drift up in pairs
looking with the eyes of the entire flock
for the way they must follow.
Sadly they call back, "No,
no, not this way. Not yet."

**5**  *Why the Blackbirds*

On the crown of the hill
legions of ruined blackbirds gather
for evening prayer. What they feel,
a blank razoring
of one song from the next,
is like a small god to me
who only sees and listens
and then puts brush down
onto the snowy breast of canvas.
The blackbirds came before anyone

can remember ever wondering
why. They came before the orange moon
or the blue sun rose out
of their cauldrons of grace and work.
They came speaking
their odd laws of the sanctity
of things which are absolute, as they
are absolutely black. They came
because the hill needed blackbirds,
I know it, leaning back, setting my paints
on a stone. They came because
nothing else would do. But why
did they stay?

## 6   *Boy in a Field*

Brown and green. Late summer
wind steady in a field of wild grass.
Walking there, hip deep, flinging stones, the boy
has recited and now recites the four principles
of love:

*That it turns the core of you to moonlight*
*That its hands are an orchard of blue secrets*
*That it is visible to the horse but not the horseman*
*That it is the only innocent bride of longing*

He weeps, this boy, hurling at a face
and a body, at a touch troubling the air.
His memory is window
jammed open on a night too lustrous for mathematics
and too short for song. In his pocket
a ribbon or photo or a loop of dark hair
calls and calls a season brushed out almost
to pure sky, like a hill in the background.

No one speaks to him or knows
his sorrow there under the tipped moon.
The night birds are part of him, maybe
they fly out of his perfect grief.

**7** *Old Man Westman and the Thistle Bird:*
*A Fragment from Arizona*

On this parched hill I think of thistle, bright
in its spiny bloom and fold. I think of thistle tea,
sweet steam of a long twilight in some place
I suppose I must be going to. It will be shady there
and none but thistles in the broad fields sing
with what will take so very long to say:
Life, I the dark bird circled with small purpose, worm
on my back spinning me out
to Earth, the gleaming-place. My bones
are there, maybe; and all my loves, leaves
of a lone birch tree aflutter in this song
the shining guest brushes with her spiky purple wing.

**8** *Portrait of Eldon Clay, Deep in Thought*

The corn will come, and enormous fireball tomatoes,
and beanstalks looking for heaven or pots of gold.
The mailman with his grey smile will come
handing out news and good wishes with the bills.
Down at Lundberg's horses will foal among wildflowers
already half-eaten by the goats.
Each day the nut-hard green blackberries will soften
a little as the season rolls over to admire itself.
And all will be what spring requires, lighting every lamp
but one. Oh spring, oh Earth my friend, my love will not
come to me down a small path between the moon and sun.
This soft spring caress in my hands, what shall I do
with it now?

## THIS IS THE NARRATOR, THIS IS I (GUESS WHO) DOWN BY THE LAKE IN THE DARKNESS

It is false
what they say of rolling stones, they gather
broken edges
and lines around the eyes.
I'm so old now, so rounded down, I sometimes think
life was what I only dreamed of waking to
after the stage went dark—or the battlefield.
I could tell you this or that, repeat
that there *were* harness bells
and that it snowed the winter Edwin
Dugan died of a drunken weeping blindness
when the ice collapsed.
That the sky was deep
and softly promising when Ellie hung
her apron on a branch
and put her mouth on me to call
the lost continent in my blood
with a gentle sucking sound.
That I lived in thirty cities after that
and none of them
was home. Misdirected, misbegot: I could tell you
none of the town's pain was my construction.
I wasn't even here—though
Ellie stayed. Poor girl, now nine years
in the gravel and never a husband
and few in scattered corners who recall
her small step among the mutilated zinnias
of local myth.
So I remember. An old piano
in a corner of my head
turns a yellowed page and spills out

"Paper Ship." It plays
for all the lost and sunken
rending their slow tongues against what ceases
and goes on
anyway. Old townsfolk, so far
from where you need to lie, rest easy
while I serve this bland remembered gift, these words
whose only healing graces drag you up
like old mysterious anchors
made of rust and love.

# MEMORY AND HEAVEN

(1997)

## ALIENATION

When the alien spoke of his planet
it was with an ache so profound
I forgot he was going to kill me.
I looked into the chrome and blue
glaciers of his eyes and said,
It's all right, I know how it is
when you're away from home,
when time and distance coalesce
like the speed of light
and freeze your heart's coordinates.

He didn't have a heart. He didn't
even have toes, but he liked the sentiment
and said I'd not be killed and eaten
after all
but only changed.
I thought how often change had seemed
the one salvation. But when he said it
I woke to the sensation of singing
under water, while air diminished, slowly,
like hope.

The creature, in his lance of a ship,
was soon the distant sparkle of alienation
itself: roads that will not converge,
singers who cannot close their mouths.
Was this the beginning? Who can say
where or when it began in him?
I just woke and there was this voice-like
distance
between myself and the things I loved.

# FOUR SOLITUDES

There were four of them
successively alone in their passage
along that road
no longer much more than an invitation to travel.
Courting the same woman
perhaps, singing into the same well

by which echo and reflection mask themselves
with what they must return,
the four of them only once passed by
those grassy hills, along that overgrown thought
between two lines of maples.

That all four were the same
man, that each of him beseeched the birds
for something simply every name forgets, that each
had grown a crippled wing and didn't know it,
can be told at last, at least. But why
follow this way, this unused valley track
among the rust of barns
and wagon wheels? "Why not," they would say.
"We're so hidden by wind we can't collect the light
that lets things live. Time follows this curve
of space, and moon swings her secret pearl
like water obeying the grain of wood. So here we are."

Nothing came of their journey; there were four,
each the same, drifting where they might
one day be imagined, awakened by the glaring
mind's eye and then the mind, probing and blinking
with wonder. That is, life is the appearance of unity
in series, whether you see

or it sees you, every time you reconstruct
its watchfulness and let the new guidon choose
the road you chose before, its trees, sounds
bear no witness
and dance heartless as rocks.
What's it all mean, I suppose. Sleeper, who's to know
the ear of the cello and the beech tree bud? I could only
kiss you if I knew which one of me you're not. It's clear
as the four of them eloping, each with Descartes
on his lips
and the supposition of loss draped over him
like a robe of power.

# THE ECSTASY OF CEASING TO KNOW

I painted my hand on the window
and that part of the glass ceased to know itself
because with windows, form is its own recognition
and the portrait of my hand was alien
formal hypothesis. When I painted
the same hand on an arm
of the blue chair, I thought I heard breathing
and for a moment supposed also a spot of lighter blue
weaving a slow ironic signature over the cushion.
But soon my disruption of the chair's being
and its subsequent brief tango at the margins of simulation
passed into the known body and fabric of CHAIR
and I fit my living hand
to the image, which remained quite helpless
before the mockery implied of this gesture.
Then I desired to paint my hand against the cat
but he discerned some pallor in the silence of my shoes
and he bolted
and even now, weeks later, remains aloof
so that I doubt the project shall engage him more directly.
Still, on a back wall of his brain a terror
strokes him, inevitably
in the shape of my hand. Well, I moved on
to the appliances
with decent though short-lived result, owing to the systematic
interference of current, a liquid presence
the praxis of which is related to singing
in the very sense in which appliances are not.
I took note of this and, cuing on the whiteness
of refrigerators in general (and of mine most particularly),
I discovered the large, flat articulation
of my hand itself *pretending* "refrigerator."

Such challenge: to simulate the intentional ellipsis of form
unintentionally conceiving only self when there is no only self!
Well, the work glides forward
furiously, in some zones; on others the photo-intimation of stasis
fingerpaints Plato with shadows palpable as rock—
which it would be possible to break up and carry away.
Therefore, clearly, no hierarchy exists between subject
and object so that not only must the hand be painted *on* its mirrored
original, it must also (I see at last) be painted *by* this same hand.
Here I have encountered a near hallelujah
of telemetric fishhooks and a piquant ignorance
for which no language serves and by which I begin, dimly, to see
that non-shape, so familiar to my cat, as a ballet
of opaque, perfected, and dozing subject/object calculations
which, yes, are (I feel it!) painting me
over and over like a pencil
drawing a cartoonist who has recently ceased to know
the shapes of humility and science as they coalesce in him
and this ecstasy is born without image or thought
of image, without hope of any kind.

## ELEGY AT THE ONSET OF WINTER

*—for James Wright*

I love you and wish you grace,
dead apple, empty space.
You were fair enough, almost blond
in any case, and I come alone
at dark to call you friend and good
deceiver of the Devil's face.
If we touched, you could come back
to be the wind-teased cottonwoods
lining the tangled field at dawn.
You could come down
from the bridge that bears you,
grey as breath, aloft
and singing like a single paper rose
because you hear the ancient palm
of light unfolding for a song
called *Whisper, Were You Ever Here?*
or where in the blinding quick
of summer have you gone?

# DIALECTIC FROM THREE WINDOWS

**1** *For the Fishermen*

Rain and gray shoulders of the sea.
I think of Jesus walking away
against the horizon, those in the boat
open-mouthed,
almost angry with astonishment.
And in the bar afterwards, of course,
he lets them tell it.
But his face is the calm water
hiding everything. "Come on, Jesus,
how do you *do* that stuff?"
He isn't saying. He just sips his wine
then water then wine
and thinks about weather in the age
to come, how dark it will be,
how far men will have to walk—and over
what water—for a good joke
or a blessing.

**2** *With the Distance*

The birds of leaves are waving
as if they had no voices.
It is their way with the distance
which has no voice
but only the shapes, sounds
of wings, footsteps, water hurrying off.
So, if I hold a bird of leaves
fluttering like a moth
in my closed hand, I will not be required
to read aloud the journey I begin to see

in your straight, strong body.
The landscape there is miles of hawthorn trees,
blossoms elegantly clothing their knives
as though beauty doesn't hurt
when we try to hold it, rocking,
waiting for the strange green birds to sing.

**3** *At Friday Harbor, Near Christmas*

On an ice and salt encrusted piling
the cormorant has been all morning
as if crucified,
drying his wings in the snow.
Black beacon to the slow bobbing
boats asleep here for months,
he is without sadness and does not know
whose loneliness clings to him
through a window across the water.

Oh one of these days
when I have shed my body, dark bird,
I will walk out to you
and sit quietly
enjoying the morning, the white dazzle
of it falling through my outstretched wings.

# BLESSING'S PRECISION

And we emerged from the tree line
and came upon a lion, bleeding
and a man kissing the wounds
from which the blood whispered out.
Some of us wanted to kill the lion
quickly, then the man
and to write down how this was done,
how a voice commanded it.
Some of us wept for the lion
and for the love the man must have felt
to bend down like that, like an angel,
and do what he was doing.
Some of us thought we could see home
in the bloody grass and in the stillness
of the man's mouth saying a thing
no one but the dying
lion was close enough to hear.

Finally we decided to make a ritual
for passing by a wounded lion and an angel
when you come upon them
by accident
and one of them is watching his heart's blood
run bitterly away, in spite of the sweetness
it had always brought before.
And so we held our faces up against the sky
and said our benedictions
and gave up each a bead
from our own red estuaries. And a caress
we might have saved
we placed in the man's palm
till his hands overflowed with little stones

smooth as a lion's ear.
Then we left the both of them there, dying
I suppose, and many of us have been speechless
since then, curiously
simplified in a kind of sunlight asleep
in a kind of shade. Since then
we have begun to build this rose,
this village of our days
where every breathing thing must be received
and tended, because mercy, now, locks our arms
out wide, and nothing, not even happiness,
is ever turned away.

## NIGHT FLIGHT LETTER TO WELDON KEES FOUND
## WADDED UP INSIDE A LUCKY STRIKE WRAPPER

I'm writing you after all these years
because people keep saying there is this
kinship of sensibility. Flying over Kansas
now, at a dizzy cloudless elevation, I can't see it.
But you with your cigarette and mustache
and your swept-back Nathanael West darkness so deeply
in love with the cynical tide of things, I can see
them OK in this book—which I admit isn't mine.
I'm your age now is another reason
I'm contacting you. Word is you jumped
at 41; and here I am
clinging to every shred of time, by God, and wondering,
Weldon, how to live,
how to stay for one more kiss
in the arms of such mystery of heart
I can't manage either. So I was a PI and a tough
character,
arguably ("Don't try me," was, anyway, always my advice).
So I loved without any particular restraint or shame.
I love you, too; does that make us similar? Did you
really jump, throw it all
into "them shark-infested waves" like a prom queen
who's gotten old? Come on,
tell me I'm wrong (all of us
must be) as Ptolemy was wrong: that is,
because the world is not logical
is it? Think
how many have died like the solitary
tapping pattern buried in Mexico City rubble for days
while the crews dug and wept?

Was it you, Weldon, lost in the hours of earth,
plummeting into the night smile
like a bird? Well, I think
you're a shit for going off like that, on purpose,
leaving us lonely for your profile, for someone
like you but older
and hopeful. Not as dead.

## STREETS

Catullus, returning late
from the "sun-drenched farmlands of Nicaea,"
saw a hook of smoke lean
to the pink goblet
fallen from a window and smashed.
It was the hook
mourning makes, he said, after
the hand has broken faith
with what it beautifully held,
after the good air
cracks its jaw against the table.
                    Then
five silent Phrygians drifted by
rowing
and scattering little boat-like meditations
from The Book Of Odd Number.
                    Then
he heard the weeper, Flavius,
banding his ankles as he tittered and wept
about mendacity
in his lover's verbs.
                    Then
Catullus thought this night swerves
like a girl loosening her robe
while one man watches
and another paces the crooked paving stones
and longs to watch. Then
Catullus was all night in the streets
lit by smoke of a step disrobed
and shattered as a precious cup
can be. Then he was another man

and another;
     bleeding like this
bleeding like this, he said. *Imagine.*
Then he let go.

## THE CONTEMPORARY THEORIST ALONE AT DUSK
## IN HIS CHAIR BY THE SEA

The peaceful agony of cats
waiting for supper on a wide bright porch
says be wordless, if you like. Zachary Taylor,
the Dalton Gang, the republic of vanished Romans
drifting in robes
down to the Tiber to observe the conjugations of late sun
on water: these are the same
silent glisten you, hand on a shut book, speak to now.
Tell it to stop implying transcendence and the shameless
presence of gods whose love is only the inexplicable
cats filled with summer light.
Tell it you've tried feeling holy when days or seasons
turn puzzled faces through the air
like random beams of Sanskrit, so pure
they translate themselves. Insist
you'll not be bled
by the vaunted longing-to-define that births such slow and ugly
necessary thoughts. You've been to the mountain, say,
and the other mountain
and they were about the same. Say, what's *here* is the strangeness
filling everything
and unable to talk about it. Of course, words are wasted
on the water, no matter how metaphorical. And naturally you'll
admit
(though not privately) its grace
is like a brother; something you never asked for,
something like you
with a language referring always and only to itself.

# TALK WITH THE MOON

*Tutto e pace e silenzio, e tutto posa*
*il mondo, e piu di lor non si ragiona.*
　　　　　*—Giacomo Leopardi*

Leopardi asked the moon if it, too, would be silent
all his life.
After the grass and stones refused his graceful inclinations
he had tacked all hope of magic to the moon because
beauty, he said, privately, is the failure of realism.
But that night when he asked
the moon was real enough
and Leopardi, looking up, turned his ankle in a rut
and low-bridged his nose against a bough that over-hung the way
he had to follow then.
He cursed, and who could blame him? I know the dazzle
and simplicity of voice he longed for
but had not wished to talk about
earlier
when his wife, tired of his pacing the house, said, "Get
the hell out of here, why don't you? Go down to the bar
with Ugo or Alessandro or Giuseppe or go up to your room
and write some poetry!"
Though he had no wife, of course,
this sword-thrust made the tang of metal bloom
on Leopardi's tongue. How could he say
to her
the soul's night vision would burn out in heat and blare
of such bonfires
banked against the ordinary cold? Well, so, playing it out,
he put on his hat with the long purple feather
and stumbled into Florentine moonlight
like a foppish drunk.

What does it matter where
he went, his puzzled up-cast face seeking a voice
and all its secret fellowship ascending
with the ancient stars?

What does it matter? He knew where he was; he opened
the door and found himself, an old poet, dead
a century and more, smiling as the moon's mouth moved
to say, "All is peace and silence, and the world
rests entirely, and we do not speak of them now."

## YOU SAILED AWAY, OH YES YOU DID
*—for Adam Hammer, 1949–1984*

Against the sky, against the water sailing away
was not as blue as snow beside a trough
from which a naked girl has stepped moments before
she is imagined. Sailing away was never so vivid
as hammer marks in the door jamb of a shed, either.
And I never saw you shining a stone on your sleeve,
dropping it into the twinkly phosphorescence.
And you didn't lunge for the throat of a new book
about esthetics and the average man who sails away
in a Ford, the last of it assembling around him
as he studies his charts and holds one finger moistly up
in windless afternoon.

Where was he sailing to? wonder the wounded mammals.
Certainly none of this occurred in Florida
or in the nautical vacancy of a stowaway's tongue
frozen by laughter. Certainly I sailed some way
with him, or you, regardless of head-on Fords
falling into the side mirror of a night average as dots.
Certainly as you sail the undressed sea
empty of owls, the grass around me is rusting, collapsing
because it is so stupidly ashore
caressing its sad laces, knowing you've gone.
Like a proton parking meter filled with mischief and stars,
like a fig bar the rain disapproves of,
like a window becoming a zip-lock bag when no one is listening,
like a man dressing his grief in a clown suit
you've gone.

# THE RECORD PLAYER

In the next room Barbara listens to ballads; familiar,
inoffensive phrasings discovered at a used record shop
on Hawthorn. The woman's voice is low and strong

with its charmed lights and losses winking and the
moon sailing off by itself somewhere above the rain
and other forms of weeping for the Earth.

Then she swings brightly south, Caribbean, where love
is a thoughtless shimmering absence of decay we think
we must, by suffering, have earned. Occasionally

she mentions cormorants and the color blue as it must
have been for Columbus, bent above his imaginary
charts, hollering at his first officer, "Not now!

Not now! Can't you see I'm plotting a course!" Finally
she brings a song of sleep and wordlessness and the
machine lifts its arm coldly out of her voice,

sinking now into the dark vinyl like a djin charmed
back into a golden lamp that isn't really gold. If the
voice returns

it will come because we call it, by devices; it will never
bring itself. In this it differs from events; the artifactual
aplomb of war, for instance,

seems avoidable only in retrospect as men in
immaculate pinstripe move among the smoking arms
and heads, counting and thinking we didn't ask

for this one, boy. We didn't even know it was inside us all this time, pretending to be a song we had grown tired of

or forgotten as we forget the moon's dark other hand, the one that points, naturally, toward the emptiness and salutes.

# THE PIPES OF OBLIVION

Nansen went up on deck and saw a bird-shaped
constellation
flying and singing as it flew.
It didn't bother him; in those days
Norwegians often saw that sort of thing.

He took out his pipe, whacked it on the rail
to clear the bowl,
then wandered aft, thinking, "What astonishing notation
the footfall brings. This must be oblivion!"
It was a giddy time,

the ice was taking them to where the North began

and it was likely they would die
(as the grim joke went) of having no place else to go.
The bird shape sang again. O well, he ordered the mate
to turn in
and stood the rest of the watch himself,

letting smoke rings lift into the icy arctic wheel
and thinking how little time
mattered
to a ship or man stuck fast
in a voyage
even imaginary gods could not recall the object of.

# EVERYTHING

Ponce de Leon, whose youth was all too short,
scrawled his name and number into the *Book
of Certain Sorrows* by wanting everything
to stay, always, just the way it no longer was.

His fine moustaches and silver mirror,
his fingers buffed like little marble candlesticks,
the heart-shaped box where he sent hope to lie
against itself, waiting out the miracle he was sure
hacked its way toward him through the mangrove swamps,
using prayer beads as navigational aids: anyone
could read the signs.
                          And he had a funny,
rounded sort of name, "Ponce," falsely intricate,
like a Swiss watch made of chocolate.
Also he was small and getting smaller
as the quest went on; three times he had his armor
taken in so that, approaching a pool or bubbling spring,
he would project that no-nonsense manly form
Indians in Florida, ever since, have known to mark
a magnitude of lunacy from which to "hush" and wink
and tippy-toe away.
                          In the end, too, he sang—
to keep his spirit tuned and ready to receive the whole
hog mysteries of never-ending day—and his men sang with him
so he wouldn't seem so mad to them
and the birds observed these clanking choristers
slogging fiercely, eyes on the sun, stooping
here and there to drink and then to wait for something
impure but better than St. Sebastian's grace, some
blessedness absolving them of knowledge
                          and of fear

for old Ponce, mad as a hatter in the lists
of dawn, who would lead without followers
if he had to, who made their loyalty a sacred hope.
Against all reason they stared him in the crazed
crossed eyes and said, here is all we have, our youth.
Not quite a fountain, but take it. Take everything.

## MEAN AND STUPID

Ricky Stoppard died
in a slimy, undulant tangle
near the south face of a strip mine
outside Wier, Kansas.
That was where the snakes
caught up to him, praying
too loudly and taking the Lord's name
at the same time.
That was how it was.
All the Baptist farmers
hereabouts will tell you
it was a low-down
two-talking son of a loafing skunk
who died that day (riddance be praised!);
that Ricky stank corn liquor,
cursed life, had once attempted armed robbery
of a charity bazaar in Girard, and that the snakes
were instruments of a judgment
others had been making for a long time before the Almighty
at last threw the machineries of balance
into gear. Rumor
has it, too, that Ricky, when he fell
into the fateful waters of reptilian vengeance,
called out for someone to toss him
a brick, thereby adding stupidity to the list of charges.
I've seen his gravestone and it reads:

RICKY STOPPARD
1953–1985
Mean & Stupid

I'm standing by that stone, and my hat is off
to his silly death
and a life of miserable small crimes
poorly made. I pray I may be spared
the pain and heat of Ricky's soul
that sighed like a rotten wagon wheel
and broke. And I pray for that
soul, the Old Nick of it somehow
near to me as love
or yearning
or any lost equation none of us will ever finally
get. I can hear the night freight
mourning through Riverton
as farmhouse lights die out
below the darker owls circling, flagrantly
disdainful of the Oklahoma line, and Ricky's cruel
headstone comes undone. He's finished now, at least,
and he's all right (being gone). The wind
and blown leaves clatter and agree, at least
he's not all wrong.

## STAY WITH ME

Beautiful arms full with rose starts,
he says a tree
or ship is not a cloudy day.
He says the way wind stains
the brief smiles of doors
is what we get from life
and nothing less or more
should we accept; not even
from strangers, the sometimes holy
and come out of nothing fools.

Who knew he was dying?
We were on the path home
when that bell removed its pearls
and flung them skyward, dozens
of little moons, whole notes, berries
full to sweetness with a song
he sang us from the atmospheres
of Christmas, where all of us are going,
blessed or not,
ready or not, like a grandpa

in a greenhouse humming
and falling into his smile
as we went down the path, away
from the unfractured life; the three
of us filling like glass
with what we were about to know:
this is no dream. Beyond cartwheels
and the slow designs in grey,

every heartbeat is a little morning
with a path and someone,
made almost inarticulate by love,
watching.

# THE CRY

The moon hangs in alders
by the bridge. Something is crying out
down there in the choked hollow,
down there in the grass. Trapped
or maybe bereft, it trumpets
up the ladders of mist and cold
as if nothing mattered anymore
except voice hefting the exact fullness
of this moment in which something
is terribly wrong.

I'm afraid of you,
whatever you are, and of your grief
or pain sung like a gift
no one will take.
Once, I think I will come down to you
through scotch broom and heaps of leaves
and put my fingers softly
to your throat and stroke you and feel
the dense shiver of language
leaving you, seeking my nameless body
somewhere outside of what we are
in daylight or in summer.
But it's autumn now and I don't want to die
or hear you, dying fascination. I don't
want the frayed rim of your call
ringing back out of my hands
and scuffling shoes. Yet you cannot
be still and the long word rasps
again onto the air.

An owl calls a few times: testing
testing. I turn toward home,
nudging aside pity, guilt, and echoes
of the suffering every creature knows.
Nothing changes what I cannot do.
This is how broken things
pile up inside of me and I keep walking,
calling out, "I love you. Come to me
because I cannot come to you."

## BROWNIE HAWKEYE

In the last columns of sunlight
holding up the roof
we stood proudly with the fish
so my mother could snap us
and give the attic shoebox this
dusky square-framed happy pittance
of 1955. You can just see
a piece of lake
reflected in my father's casting reel
attached to the pole he holds aloft
like Poseidon lifting a trident
to the powers and bounties of the sea,
that they are his.
And my father's face says
                on this
tremendous day we struck forth
over dark uncertainties
in an all but rotten boat
and reached down
and brought from the deep a glimmering
alien life
and have returned in the fullness
of our proven skill to this
green eternal shore.
          It is a shore
grey-yellow now
as I sit gazing, unable
in the vaguely silvered light to tell
if I look back at myself,
at my father beaming there,
or at the fish swinging dead
and beautiful between us.

## THE RIDE
*—for T. L.*

You probably don't remember,
it was years ago. You and I and Amorosi
and David Lyon rode down to Springfield
in the back of Tremblay's rattletrap van.
                              You sat
with a pint of peach brandy in a bag
on your knees
and said nothing
the whole loud careening way
along the back roads from Belchertown.
I thought you disdainful of us
maybe, or too drunk to know
we wanted you to speak
                    as we spoke
about the evening or the road
or the ghostly broken mill towns we passed through
or anything at all.
                    But you just sat
under your lank whitish hair,
tippling, not even looking up
when we hit the possum, all its kittens
hung from it like a string of bells.
Tremblay nearly cried, rocking
like a bear in the headlight beams,
shaking his head above that quivering
heap of blood and eyes.
You didn't get out with the rest of us
to console or lead him back
so the journey could go on.
                    When we arrived
and piled out to find the appointed room,
you said, "It's cold tonight"

to no one
and I saw my judgment of you
a broken worried thing, like so much
of what we knew then
in those days after the war.
                    You simply hadn't cared
to speak.
You had your thoughts
and the rest of us were just the rest of us
borne together through a single night,
no one knowing it would never end
and never be the same; no one but you
knowing how much the voice can cost, how wrongly
it can take you
into the path of a transfixing lie, its headlights
coming on
monstrous and too beautiful for words.

# WINDOW

I look out and think of the Brethren
of the Common Life, the love that single gestures must
have shown them as they beat against
the hard peculiarities of Groote's devotions,
and my mind passes over into Deventer,
its moat and ancient spires taking the sunlight
in which Frederick of Heilo and the good
a'Kempis stroll together in their penguinesque cloaks.
                                        Right here
the Devotio Moderna lights up its collective earnestness
as though five hundred years were glass blown out a window,
pages torn from books.
                        Again Thomas bows
before the sanctity of drovers, and shepherds and smiths:
"If you cannot sing like the nightingale
and lark, then sing like the frogs and crows, which sing each
as God intended," he says
in my room here
                on the budding and breezy plains
where I read *The Imitation of Christ* on my day off, a little
Franz Liszt for background, the active dark
of the pianist's left hand waking a scent of lemons in a Delft bowl
in some everyday life that is not mine.
                        In fact, after ages
of loving the wrong books, reading women whose syntax was ill will
itself, whose eyes, when they turned from the fire, were the shapes of fire,
even if I happened to be praying for that, I long for the lemony
precision it is supposed we finally come to.
                        But it is a long way
to the passions of the good brown scholars, pondering a beast
hemmed in by angels and the extravagance of flesh.

                    Through my window
I can see blue suggestions of the shriven life
farther from me than a cardinal can fly,
                    farther than the reach
of what we say is honesty or neighborly good hope
or some benison the redbud sprays up to the sweet air
on its knees
dreaming of Liszt, bursting with George Sand.

## EXCLUSIVITY

Orchestral September. The prime
insect quadrillion finish one movement
and crash into the next, mad
with the sexual sweetness of what they are saying.
High in darkened pin oaks
or along the dipping stems of shrubberies
they pipe an ecstasy even the moon could hear
if moon would listen once, if once
she weren't so much the queen
of purest darkness out beyond where sound can go.
So what, the moon has no crickets,
no katydids. So
the moon just watches ripples
of music rising off the lips of the atmosphere,
vaguely stroking her
gravitational tether until, saddened, she seems to burn
a little brighter. Which is what September means
to the insects. I remember
touching you, rubbing
you slowly with this brightness,
the brightness of time. You sang,
I remember, just as the night, because it is the moon's friend,
wished you to, just as the moon does
sing, though we can't hear her.
We can only feel.

# JUST WAKING

(2003)

## IF THE HOUSE

A house of solid grass and twilight
suggests itself
as I walk up a dark hill from the bridge.
If it calls me come in,
I will send it the names of women
or the name of a finch
becoming a woman
after the house is asleep, dreaming itself
deep down under my hair. If it is humming
*Lili Marlene*, from my pocket someone will answer
like a set of fingers suddenly
possessed of voice, suddenly with no language
but an absence
growing into the space between two hands
when they have let each other go.
If the house of grass and twilight
becomes for a moment my grandmother
rising before dawn
to peer in at her children, I will offer
every good thing I have not become
and my face spattered with starlight
and my shoes slowly climbing into the Earth
looking for home.
And if the house shimmers and becomes
my love beckoning, I will set free every door
and call to her, "Come in, come in, all of this
is my mouth, my arms
lonely for you, walking up a dark hill."

# THE FUGITIVE LOVER SAYS "I'M TELLING YOU"

I tell you about the night
because it's good to love
something, even if it's darkness
and the quiet talk of leaves
and the way stars seem to lean
nearer then away
beyond the hat-like clouds.
I've never met you, of course,
and there isn't maybe
much reason you should care
or listen
but I've been out, again,
walking and musing around the old strip mine
that is the lake
in my town
and sitting a dark bench in shadows
while heat lightning blanched the sky
up toward Nebraska like a battle
seen from great distance, but silent, a spectacle
of most quiet light.
Really
you'd marvel, I think, how good it is
to smoke and watch the loneliness lift
and pass away like nagging pain
that drifts to sleep.
You'd be amazed
at the rich familiar ripples on the lake,
ducks passing through in file
(with all the urgency of brick)
and the talk of lovers and friends
on the far banks
out of sight, how it slides

exactly as ripples
on the general waves of air.
And these crickets pipe *so* clear
among the other murmured musics
you'd love them like the things you've wanted
finally here, finally peeling off
the robes of blindingness
such things always wear until, sick
of our foolishness, we give them up.
And you'd like it
when Catullus comes and I say,
"Man, what it is?"
which cracks him up
and he lights my cigar and says,
"*glubit magnanimi Remi nepotes,* Sport."
And I laugh and turn to you, "Where
does he get this stuff?"
Then there is the kind of talk you'd like,
I know.
My good dead friend Lew
shows up for a phrase, Catullus chiding us
both about our century that couldn't sort
a decent revel from a heap of leaves
and saying, "At least we *knew* most fun
is a disaster, most love
a reeking smoke." And then with his eyes
we see
off in the night air
a girl leading a blind horse out
under the snowy starlight
and it's Claudia,
of course,
the loss of whom betrayed his poems
down twenty saddened centuries of shattered heart.
And we watch her ride

into deep dazzle of the fields, alone,
and none of the adulteries or lies
can matter anymore. "Catullus,
Catullus," we say, "It's all right; the pain
is only love and wisdom finally
bursting through our heads! Have
a drink," because you've brought a bottle
if you're here
and we pass it 'round and sing
*The Old Grey Mare* or something worse
a time or two before the winking silver
night beams say it's time to go.

It's silly but I hope we link our arms
and sway
in a communion that is like love everywhere
and is the best we get
in this the only life
on this the only gleaming green blue rock
in all of howling space.
And I hope you'll know when I say "Bless"
it's you I speak for too, if you'll allow,
and for the other two already singing
as they saunter into time. I guess
I'll mean "forgive me" too. Forgive us
all
for troth broken and for love betrayed,
though it was all just human luck
or wasn't
it's all right. All night
the four of us like a necklace of odd stones
talking toward home.

## HERE IN A PROVIDENT STILLNESS

In the green spell of my window
things accept their shadows and latent forms.
For example, in a field three Confederate soldiers
sleep under a single blanket. With their wounds
exposed, we would know where to wish them
covered from the cold. As it is they are bandaged
with unwritten letters to *Miss Darcy Livenfall,*
*My Dearest Bessy,* and *Most Beloved Mother.*
The moon pours a little liquor on their brows, stilling
the iron violin of an army's anguish and exhaustion
after a defeat. A chopper
passes over the wistfulness of horses grazing
near a barn collapsed
under the thumbnail of history, its whole hand
shaking as I shake
when I turn out my light and imagine all I once knew.
My name, for instance, and where it might lead.
My father, for instance, and his father who walked
to Oregon from Kansas for the 1902 Exposition
and never went back
because how could he, having seen such wonders,
machines that ate the earth
like candy, immense trees older than Christendom,
rivers so wide and blue they burned your eyes?
Not even the Daultons laid out like rabbits
in a Coffeyville storefront meant much to him then,
though *I* see them now, as he did, gravely delicate
in their frock coats, moustaches, and bullet holes,
dreaming like so many soldiers in a field
where, in the distance, a dim coughing of spades

wanders like cordite fog
and my grandfather stops a moment in the stillness
to listen for my step and light dims and brightens
like breath.

## LIKE FEELINGS

Moonlight is all over the sycamores
and down the street singing
like a drunk.
It's all over my dog and me, too,
stepping out our evening's amble
among the crickets and parked cars,
couples murmuring on porch swings.
It is fifteen years
we've been walking the night streets
pleasantly fried by dreams lifting
everywhere along the elm boughs
and it is inside us now
like feelings
that bloom open as we move
so that finally we are out of reckoning
smoothly
richly filled, like jars, with all our nights
and walks together
and nothing spills or shatters this.
An angry shadow from an alley leaps
and shoots us
and we just step out of our bodies
and go on.

"That's life,
thank God" (mine and the god of dogs) I don't
tell him, or you, or anyone.
And I don't say I've got the pain of it
shut off or that I've buried my last
deceit. After all, it's just the dog
listening
as things gleam and lumber in the rows

of darknesses, and what *is* there to say
to him?
I could unhinge the old saw
about the sanctity of moments.
I could promise him a bone when we get back
then break my promise just to show
the waywardness of speech and truth.

Or I could tell him love is like the air
sometimes
(and vice versa), which is to say, all there is
to live on.
But he knows that.

# TWO POEMS WITH DEATH BETWIXT
*—for Bill Howell (1918–1996)*

### 1  *The Good Clouds*

My father sits alone in his boat.
    It is raining
and the fish, looking up through

their pixilated roof, aren't biting
    so he gazes
across to the misty tree-lined shore

from which a great blue heron gazes
    back, his whole
body vagely telescopic. Nothing's moving

anywhere, no other boats, it seems
    even the river
has nowhere to go. He's so perfectly,

uniquely right, hunched down just
    the way the eye
wants him as it catches the slant

and spirit of this raining day
    that began at four
with coffee and a last loving glance

at his bait supplies and tackle. If, as is said,
    the Buddha shoved off
and found satori by forgetting both shores,

then the water, wind, light, time
     and being,
he must have been a fisherman adrift

in a small grey boat awash with rain,
     blowing softly
over a steaming cup while water
     ran off his hat.

## 2 *Sailing Away*

Today,
beyond the arms of the jetty,
past the flame-colored outer marker,
my father sailed out, smiling, not lost
and not asleep. If he drifts
the current takes him as wind
will lift the birds, as a bend in the road
defines the road. He has bait and sun
enough, and he's alone and happily
reminiscent as the tide that bears him on.

Last sighted, he sat astern, raising his
thermos cup as though
in salute
to the luxuriant and dimming land.
If, waving, I call out I love him
he cannot hear. So I float this off after
his low, bright form just cresting the lip
of the known world. Good luck, I say,
letting it go, and for a moment see him
so close and clear again I raise my hand
like a kind of flag over this country
of the left behind.

Odd that he should eat grapes
at such a time, but there they are, large
and purple as struck thumbs, a little bit
of Earth's bounty for the voyage. And
in the gathering blackness, a few stars.

# HE THINKS OF THE SEA

—*for Aaron Sherman*

*Nothing is left out, not the wing beats*
*I once thought were the mystical impulse*
*toward flight, nor my first girl's worn red*
*coat smelling vaguely of rain, nor the truth*
*which is that time is not like the sea, containing*
*and giving over and taking back. It is the sea.*

\*

If the bent and wiry fisherman sets out
in his black screech of a boat, perhaps
at the edge of dawn,
he straightens into that breeze off the point
and throttles down toward a familiar
loneliness he knows as rest. Few stars
and the moon just diving down

hand him his watch and chain as the chop
kicks up and lamps wake along the shore.
Is he going home or into the panic distances
of angel-shaped spray? He couldn't say
at this nerve point of departure
where he always flicks on the pump
and zips his slicker, where he gazes

into that first glare off the sea
like an old hero who's forgotten why
anything at all was
necessary, even his charts or the squint
that brings his mouth to a kind of smile. He's eloping
with himself. If his loves are with him, if his days
return, he lets them

drift astern.
He and the great day and the sea
give their ancient and ambiguous permission
to a sound like engines and the deep green
breathing that carries us away.

## THE TREETOP MOLE


He thinks God could be right
up there, a cloud
of honey-scented and undwindling hours.
But how did a star-nosed mole's sleek
shoulders come to be
among the upper boughs
when all his life long lies with roots
and fecund swamps of soil?
Or is this blue he's waving in
a kind of soil, a fearlessness
around the ears
past which the astonished starlings peel
like meteors?
I think of the Slovak story of a prince
who took to begging, for sport,
and, as fate's pure acknowledgment, became
the angel of abandoned shrines.
So I should look for meaning
on blank roads a mole once made
under the burning field?

Through my spyglass I can see him
clinging in the sway, blinking his puzzlement
and odd resolve. He has reached the topmost
tassels, toward which all kingdoms inside of me and out
sniff and plead and blindly raise their snouts. I think
he thinks he could beg or pray for time
to tunnel up beyond the spell that measures life
by weight or truth, but his voice in me says
Well,
up here, perversely elevate, I'm not starlight or sky
or the moon's old didgeridoo. I am

myself, in tall distinction of a zone I did not make
but only found by reversal of the main
design. What's it to you if I die
and never descend? I am a dark and longing thing
and not your kind.

# THE DOVE

For weeks we had been looking for land,
driving the ship like a spear, when a dove
flopped out of the sky, exhausted, onto the fantail.
It bore no olive sprig, of course, was grey
and half-plucked and weather-torn
as a coastal pine; but we took it in. Why not?
Eat it in a pinch, anyway, and its still
green eye said it knew that
and could accept such knowledge for a little rest.
We were two-hundred miles S. SW. of the Azores,
or so we thought. And Barlow said it was for sure
a Newfoundland pigeon and had had a prodigious
hard flapping time of it, despite the summer mildness.
After some water and cracked wheat and two days' rest
we thought he would surely fly again, but he stayed,
strutting and cooing and fouling our decks
with his scorched white plastic-seeming shit.
We called him Farouk for the way he strutted and clearly
thought himself lucky and rich to have found
this floating island, teeming with suckers and food.
In squalls we kept him below in an orange crate
where he would plummet immediately into the pigeon
unconscious, dove dreamland. Perhaps he could fly
the entire vessel then, soar high over the spume
and pitching moil. We could feel the force of that possibility
as he slept, and when he woke in the calm
we thanked him; though, after the last big one, it seemed
we were lost forever, rigging a shambles, instruments in splinters,
nothing but ice-green endlessness in all directions.
We would be years on the sea, we thought, finally, unless
we kill this pigeon.

But we didn't kill him and rumor of a shore
came to rest within us like blossoms nothing rescues
from the breeze, like a darkly joyous bird asleep
and dreaming of a bird.

## NEFERTITI

Solid stone, you're farther down the lists of solitude
than most dead men I know.
A boy, I sang my lumpy songs for you
in the dank library room they kept you in to keep exactly
the lost queen that you are. You never wavered once
or cared a young toad spoke and spoke
the elongated beauty of your face
suspended on a neck no one hopes to hold
or have, ever. You did not care the miracle of dim cows
that were stone and flesh and stone
still lived in ripe fields beyond the town.
And it was not a bad town, don't punish it with love,
that broken blade of flatcars
or strung together barges of the prince, defying time.
Just *be* dead, if you like it
well enough. All the piety and fever of we who live
reneges on promises only gardens hum about.
Therefore I love you. Therefore I don't care
who hears me want the cool persuading fingers
of a better night. The better nights are never now,
cold queen of the hopeful who despair—an ugly sight.
And everything they say of you is gilt
with doubt. You're like a painted fire that lights us anyway
and drives down night's lookalike, butchering our simple
scarlet core. He's had a care for your heart, too,
and I'm amazed your burning goes on in the cold, amazed
to walk these streets that are so bent and strange with time
immeasurable
staring back down your gaze.

# THROUGH LIGHT RAIN I WAVE GOODBYE

*—for William Stafford, 1914–1993*

Elongated bell-flutes of a train
blow through my sleep, leaving tracks
and ragged men with bed rolls slung
like banjos on their backs. They're going
somewhere, all these years at the hour
before doves mourn what was, once, the sea
with its wavering small stars and choruses
of perfect night.

I'm awake now and by those shores
waiting for my friend who has gone on
over oceans of train and prairie dark awash
with lamps. "Now we give you back
the twinkling world," they say.
"Now we walk beside you like a tune
or sack packed simply
with little articles of praise."

Ah, here he comes toward me whistling
a little, waving to something the air believes
and smiling to think it might be true.

## CLOSE TO THE VEIN

Close to the vein
it's peaceful. The little boats there
waiting for nerve or lilies
are the particular spurs of shadow
I loved when no one had to know
because everything was young and
      bloom.
It was those little unroomed absences
of light that first whispered, "Secret
secret places are the sacraments of time."
I put my hands, once, in
and tried to cup the spirit of that shady voice
out to daylight. The shriek
      of it
slammed like a keyboard cover on the hands:
"No! There are friendships that end
darker than an edge of axe,
darker than steam in the midnights of ruined cities,
darker than sea shells,
darker than
      hope,
darker than the darkest things
you say." Then the voice departed and I grew
up close to the vein
where these little boats bump and turn on their stalks
like stars or luck or something I've remembered
before I
      know.

## AT JAMES ISLAND, EARLY JUNE

*—for Richard Morgan*

Green and bright and quiet as a child asleep,
the water nudges gravel slanting down from
piney woods. Beyond, ridges thrust up on three
sides as we bob at anchor in the cove, a tiny
glass mistake just waking.
                          The halyards
clank like Chinese bells announcing messengers
from the East whose golden mounts stamp
and shudder, still half covered with morning
in the cold courtyard.
                          A gull drifts close
astern and cocks his head. I hope it is the white
blue sky he listens for, because this solitude
I wanted lets the rigging tap its flattened
music out and brings no word to gull
or the grey seal pondering what I might be.
What might I be?
                          Leaning back as the young
day discards her robe, I feel the boat
ride silky up a swell and a great
heron squawks and lifts on monumental wings
to let the wave wash under him onto a point
that forms the harbor's northern arm.
                          A ship, big as my life,
is passing down Rosario Strait, bound for the high
blue sea.

So long, I say.

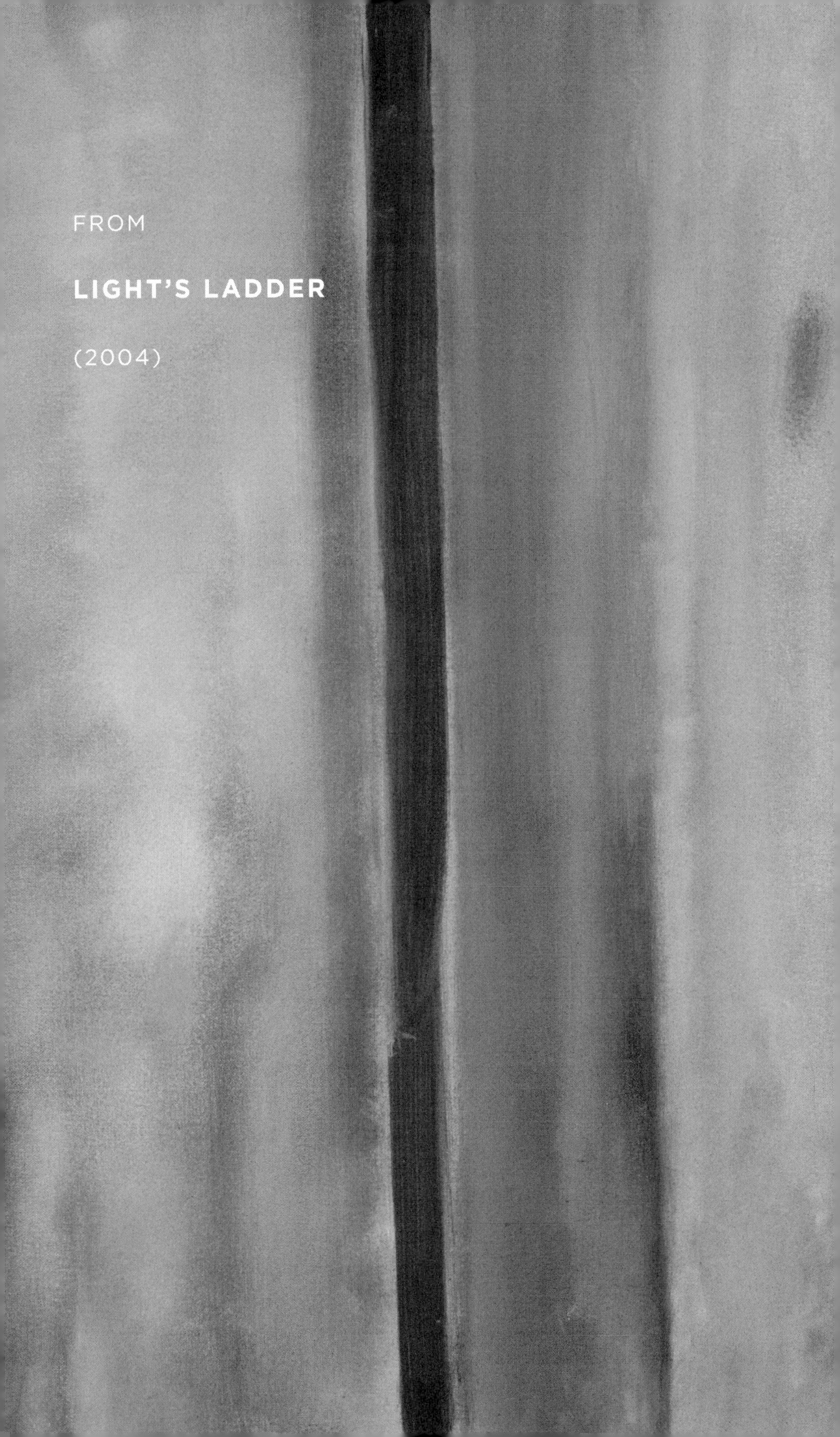

FROM

# LIGHT'S LADDER

(2004)

# IF HE REMEMBERS JUNE LIGHT IN OSLO

There was broken glass,
of course, and people were dying
as they do every minute. But, he thought,
Heaven must be this long arriving
and eternal day. So he had a beer
at an outdoor joint on Karl Johan Gaten
and thought of Hamsun starving
and of pale, dark-eyed women
who said, in that beautiful tongue, "yes,
come in," who were, even then, saying it
from opening doorways all over town.
In the palace garden

six couples were dancing under the viola
sweetness of the king's lilac trees.
Something swayed in him

as he walked near and heard the music
of their clothes dismantling restraint,
their voices becoming doves and melodies
of the body. Years from there he would remember
the freedom of his loneliness then, strangerhood
wearing him like shoes that said Listen,
there will be many likenesses
of you and many many nights, but this daylight
shall be the soul's only fragrance.
And if he remembers now
he is in love, which is the soul's condition, and alone
because that is how we live.

# RUNNING

*Orange-yellow almost kite-sized leaves whispered their*
*descent, everything falling or hanging on through the taste*
*of woodsmoke and the damp vacant lots shiny with bent-down weeds.*
*I was there because my daily ten-mile path passed that way*
*under the immense grey forehead of October sky.*

That was all. So when the dog came on
like a golden javelin clearing the wire fence,
I mistook him for a messenger of joy
and slowed to greet him
as Jacob must have turned from his quest to greet the angel
among thornbrakes and crying desert lightness.

But when the blur of him came, coiling for the flight
up to my throat,
I scooped the nearest stone and drilled it with the skill
terror lends
so that he fell from mid-air like Pegasus shot through the heart.

Screeching and foaming with adrenaline and fear, I trampled
the body and kicked it into roadside grass and gravel.
When I saw, standing by the gate, the little girl, her soundless
swollen grief, fishhooks twisting in the way
she stood, it was too late. Buttered with blood and fur, I cursed her
and ran off along the Spanaway Loop.

Each year at this time
the child, thirty-five now at least, wakes me
with her reddened watery voice.
And each year I sever my legs or carve
out my heart that she shall not have seen that day
the dancing bestial fact of skull,

fur, wings, everything
done to ruby dust.

                    He was just protecting me, she says
in a little ghost voice, and you come along and send him
straight back to heaven
           like a bird.


There was no pleasure in it, none, I plead (lying
like so many others, about the wanton peace that comes
with killing), it was fear he might have torn me like a doll,
sawdust trickling out onto the sodden road, all my hope just pennies
thrown away.
                  She lifts her arms then
and shows the signatures of blades, tongs, fists, and common
sorrow, badges
of her ravishments. And, placing my fingers in the scars, she
does a little crow-like step and sings

              O happy life that's like the sun,
              Come out come out, the burning's done.


Then I beg her flay me like a fish, down to the gleaming
soul, but she's gone and taken a spider's face, the many eyes
tearless, weaving an unremembrance that will not catch or hold
even the smallest essence of the years through which I fall
and go on running.

## TRUSTING THE BEADS

No matter what I longed for, it seemed the sea
was all there was, if you didn't count moon
and shark fins
in our wake, glittering with phosphorescence like narrow
intimations of defeat.
Even so, there was no news but the war
and unaccented rumors
of what women left ashore might choose to do.

George's wife rode off
on a Harley
and never sent even the poisoned "Dear George" we just knew
was coming for us all.
                        But blossom
begets blossom, I believed, and any breeze could be
a messenger of hope.
About my wife, therefore, I ventured to suppose
So what
if she furgles till her teeth dissolve?
So what if I die
and my body, "committed to the deep," never knows again
the silken suffrage of her skin?

Cloud shadow mingled with the bright
and salt.
The soaring albatross held to its course like Saint Brendan
trusting his beads
as a kind of chart by which intention grew into the actual
New World, forever arrived at and then
destroyed.
                        And sometimes, I confess, I ground my teeth
and spat, God help her

when they let me off this tub.
                              And then I thought, again,
So what?
We're all sailing off the edge like towers on a conveyor
to the blue
glow of snuffed out candle smoke.
Have any of us loved enough
if love is all we have?


                    Sometimes
when the wind was up and the ship lifting and plunging
like the men
who were surely sleeping with our wives,
I stood rocking
on the fantail, tearing official documents into flowers:
pay voucher roses,
requisition pinks,
leave-request lilies
fluttered over the rail and sank like votes.
Once I tossed
a typewriter and got twelve days in the brig.

At Mast, "What's the matter with you, son?" the XO asked.
"What's wrong
with the whole goddam bunch of you?"
Smartassed,
I told him it had to do with style, but it didn't.

On and on we steamed, Sisyphian, the marriages going down sordidly
in flame, grief's aftermath
shrouding the ship like haze above a village
smoldering in rain.
What was wrong would have scarred the fish-like stars and turned our decks
to soot

had it unmasked itself. What was wrong was a Hitler mannequin's
design, all of us
in rows but drifting, saluting a scrap of cloth, red-white-and-blue wreckage
behind us everywhere,
and the old New World a navigational distortion found by faith alone,
as Luther said
about salvation. But we were faithless, as our wives
must have known
and dull, almost mean, with the shame of that.

# HISTORY

At Agincourt King Henry said, "First
bastard who runs gets his jewels
on a plate," or words to that effect.
His sidekick the Duke of Gloucester
remarked some movement of the birds
in a spinney of winter birches off
to the left. Several men farted
into the pre-combat silence. Archers
on the flanks were cracking wise about
the Queen's fey scribe sent along to write
the whole thing up. There was more
farting because some of the horses
had died and the men had eaten them
to the very great distressing of their bowels.

All night it had rained as the archers
drove a bristling breastwork of sharpened
stakes that fuzzily chivalric Frenchmen
would later try to charge through
on their blindered and caparisoned war steeds.
The horse meat was raw and muddy;
though some of it, men swore, was served
by fluffy angels in blue hats. In the soup
of rain and dung and ploughed ground, those
who could sleep had thrown down in full
armor against inclines of the cold ditches.
Some whores from the village came round
but the priests ran them off—both facts
left out of the scribe's sensible and fervid
battle piece scrawled on bleached mule hide
and holed up, now, in a vault in the British
Museum.

Anyway, it was the moment before
the first French charge, after the giggling
archers had drawn back their ashwood bows
and rained a six-thousand-shaft volley onto
the noble armored heads of the Gallic cavalry,
deafening hail of ball bearings on a tin roof.
Things were quiet as could be then
for everyone, after the ringing stopped,
when up out of nowhere flew a clutch of white
doves, which circled three times between
the two poised belligerents in array and,
in the scribe's telling, "a-cryed out as one
voyse fore to taken eych mann merci on hys
enymys. And thyr was much astonyshment
befor the charage."

Later, after the wildly retreating French
horse had collided with their own infantry
tottering headlong the other way, after the English
archers had laid down their bows
and with giant mallets set to the beturtled
knights in all their shit-stained iron, someone
remarked the birds again
turned mute, crow-like and aimless as playbills
fluttering from the darkened galleries
of the next six-hundred years.

# IF THE WORLD WERE GLASS

We'd all be windows for the silicone
swallows to fly through or break
their necks against, like the grosbeaks
in Corvallis, years ago. I'd be addressing
the vacant, upturned faces of the dinner plates
and bonk! this lovely green and black corpse,
wire-like toes askew, on the window ledge.

If the world were glass, some of us might
*be* window ledges where pigeons would
leave their little glass excreta like dirty beads
and tormented solid glass jumpers agonize
briefly before stepping out
onto the shattering air, where peepers
just as agonized would edge along
for a clearer view of glass women
in their gleamingly transparent glory.

Everything would be as it is
if the world were glass. It would be
difficult to actually see others, and hard
to go home because of confused notions
of the light, and distances magnified out of
all those proportions by which we had hoped
to live. Often the voice would crack or the heart
collapse in a heap of tailings and ineffectual
repair.

Often, in so much glare and music, we
would not know where to turn
for love, or anything else
and our great heroes would be those
who simply would not break.

# A PARTY ON THE WAY TO ROME

In rouge of the night lanterns
I saw four of them rise, one trailing
a blanket, and steal to a bunk near
where I pretended sleep.
Beyond bulkheads and decks the sea
was a rushing dirge by which they cast
that blanket over the man there and began
to hit, hissing "How's this you fucking
faggot shit!"

Most of us little more than boys, taken off
to war in the usual way, lay listening
to the curses and the cries.

When they were done, Chuck, the leader, saw me
watching and could not clear his face of angry, shamed
confusion, a man caught between what was
and what was wrong. Meanwhile
the beaten one began to scream, "You let them
do it, you just let them!" Then he went weeping
and bleeding up the ladder, the compartment behind him
quiet as a burned out church.

When the MAA, taking his time, came among us,
his flashlight could not wake a single witness
so he left, shrugging, promising Justice.

Aeneas endured the distant smoke he knew was Dido
burning. *Poor wench.* But nothing could sway him
from the path appointed. That is, the free
right life, even the very fruits of empire, was not
so far or difficult to reach, we knew, if one held

steady, unnoticed and on course, if one obeyed
necessity's goddess and could pay
with the kind of fear that pleased her. So smoke
drifted
beyond horizon's palpable secret and nothing more
came of it. So on our very own ship a man
had dared not to sail from whatever called him
master of the undivided self.
So he had loved men,
it was more than you could say
for the rest of us.

## THE COUNTERCHIME

One night with my lover
and her husband
when I did not know how it would end,
I stood by a window in the house we seemed to share
and saw Lake Union glittering with anchor lights.
I was almost back from the war.
I felt like Odysseus
looking down at the campfires and ships, Troy
smoldering behind him, Achilles,
Patroclus, Ajax dead and gone.
He was weary and at peace with rapine,
loot, and murder, believing the gods
had played out their vicious game at last,
that he could walk right down to the sea
and shove off. Any time, he said, wind
or no wind. Row it if he had to. In a far room
the radio was playing some big band
swing and each of us at our separate stations
felt the saxophone lightness that assumes
both death and Fred Astaire. Probably
Odysseus heard flutes, lyres, someone singing.
Some geese passed, way up under the starlight, calling,
exactly on course for home. That was years
and years ago. Odysseus
would be home by now, slaughtering the suitors
and reclaiming his patient spider who wove
and unwove passion in the name of love.
Tennyson would think of him later, by the shore,
kicking stones and sighs into the cobalt Aegean.
Still later, at his desk, the poet heard his hero's
breathing, got up and stirred the fire
and read over what he'd written. He knew others

near and far lay tightly bound to bliss. The gods
were fast aslumber, Odysseus dead
and in the Happy Isles, perhaps. Oh well, he thought
of the vast oceans of the yet-to-be, blew out
his candle and turned away from the window as I would
decades down the line. Things were wrong for me then.
It was a long way home and nothing migratory
about it. Spending my love
like another man's money, I could have written
*The Dystopiad of Everyday Life*. I could have
rowed out on the black dazzle, trusting to fate
and the strength of my bow
bent back like the counterchime of Tennyson's footfall
as he "trod the stair" in that house
where I would some day imagine him thinking
there is too much grace in language, really, even tricky
Odysseus knew. But I stayed where I was
by the shore
and woke in a scum of cordage and ashes.
If my boat was there, I missed it
and the war was over and all of us
were gone.

## 1974

California was burnt sienna almost the whole
way up winter's rock-strewn coast
to the Redwoods
where, when the acid wore off, we slept.
All night towering voices bent
over us the language of a choir before it sings
and the memory of it after.

                        In the morning
we did not know who we were, blinking
and staggering, the sun occasionally blue
or darkened with faces. Once I saw
my grandfather hoeing in a field of trees. Frost fell
like glitter out of the reaches
until we thought, "This world needs none
of the likes of us among all these titanic
flags." Something like that, a small thought
yawing out of us bird-like and perfectly
alone. Then the truck refused to start
and we slept again.
                    Twenty-four
years ago.

                 Sometimes life is the cold edge
of a morning moon
still silver dollar bright and almost never going down.
And sometimes in that light
                              grandfathers
straighten and look back through bare limbs
of the orchard to tell you something's been lost,
something you're lonely for.

## HE WRITES TO THE SOUL

I'm just jotting this note so you won't forget
that though life is blue behind me and stony
in the instants I pause for, I have beads and shells
enough to hold back a sidelong toppling. Anyway,
at every crossing I kneel and say "Excelsior!"
and light a little fire in a jar and drink it down,
hoping if fire's a prayer no one will answer it just yet.
But I guess that's clear. At first I thought I'd write you
about the hemp-trap roses that grow by collapsing
and bringing home whatever's trying to sniff them
at the time, about what that means. Then I thought
that's just peering at the innards of luck, and no good
comes of such haruspicy. So I guess I'll give you
news about the lake dark which is growing, too,
and just yesterday began working up into the sky
among softball and badminton of the angels.
Lucky they were already wearing headlamps
to bedazzle the fish up there! Lucky their suede rings
keep their hands afloat, otherwise who knows
how they'd copy down the braille God keeps sending
like flocks of perforated swans? Some good news is
the apple tornadoes are out of blossom now
and have become zinc, which as you know
says very little and requires practically no disaster.
That's what Mom says, anyway, and she should know.
She says she knows about you, too. She says
you are the shade of something folded and alone
on a long leash of red pearls and that God
put you there because he couldn't help it.
But I don't know, I think you're somehow related
to this lake . . . like its language maybe, or like the idea
of swimming, which I've always enjoyed. Well, that's it,

I guess. Don't fret about my safety; if the weather
doesn't suck its trigger finger while it hunts for time,
or if something huge and golden lets me have its keys,
I'll be OK. Lake or no lake, some days I feel
perfectly disguised in front of you, like intention
around an iceberg or sunlight on the skin of the rain.
And I'm happy now, happy as a jungle, happy as a wisp
of dreaming melon and I cry only on your days off.

# KING OF THE BUTTERFLIES

In the last days of the reign of John II Casimir,
King of Poland, it was decreed that two million
butterflies, 100,000 for each of his years
upon the throne, should be captured and sent up
to God, an offering of the Earth's bounty in praise
of His role in the establishment of true regality.
Thousands of peasants were set to the construction
of nets and the most delicate snares so that each
lovely animal could be brought perfect and alive
to the grace of sacrifice. Blackguards and blasphemers
were released from gaol, promised royal pardons
and gold should each deliver within seven days 1,000
of the brilliant fliers to Korbecki, Chancellor
of the Realm, Keeper of Keys and Lists.
Those who brought moths by mistake were impaled
and left to die screaming outside the Palace of Justice.
Those who brought dead or damaged goods were forced
to eat them, then to wrestle the King's bull, Njok,
whose hoofs were razors and who had never been bested.

Frequently the butterflies were brought in little cages
such as one might build to house a cricket or a god
of those slim shadows wavering in out-of-the-way elbows
of a pondside path. An entire corner of the King's
garden, jammed with nectar-bearing blossom, was netted
to contain the fluttering magnificence which, as the insects
grew in number, came more and more to resemble
a single dazzling existence, moving in undulant, serpentine
iridescence below the terrace where the King would
sometimes stand rubbing his hands as he watched.

On the seventh day the counters declared their collection
still 176,314 butterflies shy of numerical fulfillment,
which fact the Chancellor tremblingly reported to His
Majesty, who forgave him this failure and awarded him
three hours to make up the shortfall
or else.

Korbecki ran from the presence and pressed
virtually everyone he met into his personal service,
sending flocks of searchers into the meads
laden with cages and nets and nectarly enticements. The last
pennies of his fortune he spent bribing the counters (a small
army of dwarves in lace gloves) to announce that a sufficiency
of butterflies had at last been obtained. They took his money
but declined. Peasant after peasant returned with single
white admirals, or with woodland graylings almost
too small to be counted.

"What is happened, dear God?" Korbecki pleaded aloud,
at which words an old chandler approaching with a large
spotted fritillary in a reed cage said, "Excellency,
you have already nearly all the butterflies in Poland.
Would you have us bring Russian butterflies? Lithuanian
butterflies? Butterflies who do not even know our language?
Of course you would not! But happily, Sire," he said
smiling, "I have captured the King of all Polish butterflies!"
Korbecki briefly considered having the man dismembered
and fed to the royal goldfish, but instead, taking a wild chance,
bent to the little cage and spoke to the fritillary, "Oh
small but mighty one, how may I find, within the meadow
of an hour, 170,000 of your most beautiful brethren?"
And in a melodious voice the King of Polish butterflies
replied, "I have heard of this foolishness and, as you see,
have myself been caught in it. If you release me, I will send

what you desire, but this sacrifice," he said with the shadow
of a laugh, "will be quite impossible and will cost you
your life."

"If you do not send them," said the suddenly weary
and no longer astonished by anything Korbecki, "my life is forfeit,
in any case." And he opened the cage saying, "Gather them, then."
And the bright creature flew off toward the forests.

Twenty minutes later a blizzard of color blew out of a cloud
and descended on the gatherers who plucked them, tenderly, every
one. And when the last painted lady was tipped into the enclosure,
huge crowds assembled to watch the sacrifice proceed
and were stunned into silence by the beauty of the swarm,
by the fragrance of the wind which two million sets of wings
brought to them. And when the King of Poland ordered Korbecki
to torch the enclosure, to send up to God the splendor of his
Kingdom's butterflies in the form of smoke, Korbecki
wept and could not be brought to do it and the King had him torn
and eaten by wild pigs. And when the next chancellor also refused,
the King had molten lead poured into his ears and anus. When
a third still refused, the King raged and took up the torch
himself and marched to the immense cauldron of wheeling color,
and, finding even himself unable to take so much beauty
from the world, he cut the netting and the butterflies surged up
like an explosion of confetti, like all the world's flowers
flung into the arms of God. And the King perceived
that this tribute was acceptable and complete.

It was June 1, in the year 1668. The next day John II Casimir
abdicated the throne and was carried off weeping and broken
in a cage of silver roses.

# THE FIRE ELEGIES

### 1 *Family Values*

A man sprints to his burning house
with a tin cup full of water
and casts it savagely into huge
flames rising up like birds
or resurrected souls of a choir.
And then he stands, cup dangling
from a finger, and knows that having
fed on him like this, the world will
for awhile forgive his little
life, and he will pity even the earnest
neighbors with their casseroles and cakes.
But his wife's weeping, pointing laughter, crazed
solitude of the children imagining
poached goldfish, parakeets
black and small as nails: no answering these,
he knows, and nothing to do but run
back down the hill with that tin cup
whistling against the last good breeze
of summer, and dip it
in the moonstruck creek and run
again, carefully, up hope's incline
toward the flames.

### 2 *The Double Suicide of Marriage*

The aspen were shivering as they do
because of cold sunlight at the edge of such
vastness. And various agencies made truth
opaque, in that way the soft whiteness
of sleeping crows is invisible. A few

rocks fell into the distances of sound
announcing some things ended
and some corrections worked loose
of the plainest, most honest face.

Discarding all stories, we found it

giddy to climb alone
up the bare thigh of an incline, beyond
handholds and restraints, beyond a Jack
London-like blaze and the ukulele musings
of minds gone starkly quiet in the high
eternities of cold. It was a long
way down. We held each other's breath
and launched out cleanly into air, one word
at a time shaking like golden leaves, like fire.

**3** *To Build A Fire*

I build it like a dwelling for the spirit
of a bird, and set the skirts alight
and lean down, kissing the spark until it flares
like thought of someone sweetly gone
but appearing now
through a window in the flames.

Cadet Pilot Terry undrowns there.
All four of my grandparents
hop around in their smiles
and a beloved dog flickers to life, running mad
with happiness after rabbits too slow to be true.
There the loose bomb does not blossom

just aft of the #3 elevator so that Mel Quinner

does not rain down on us like one
of the seven plagues and I am not ordered to type, "Dear
Mr. and Mrs. Quinner, words cannot express. . . ."
And there in the flames Hendrie, at his ease,
tends geraniums and cigarettes and forty dollar gin.

What am I bid for this lens on what's missing
and what hurts? Imagine you're St. Joan
embracing the screech, dancing as flesh
peels away and you translate to smoky sky,
a wheel refracted out of time. What am I bid
for the care and horror of those onlookers

who thought they knew what fire was for?
If it's only memory and can't burn you, still
we are each of us combustibly alone, so listen,
here's the deal: at the end a sudden spirit
flies from everyone to everyone, calling names,
burning bright with this knowledge that fire
is what we're made for, that all our lives we've
built this pyre of missing parts that we've become.

**4** *Storm*

The snow pours down from immense grey buckets,
obscuring the shadows of trees.
A mailman sails past like a gun-blue blanket
scattering love letters and bills.
At the bird feeder five squirrels screech and posture
over thieving rights and cars are lost
blind things nosing all directions, trumpeting sadly
or snarling with repressed violence. The familiar
is become an outsized wedding cake of chilled
strangeness for which nothing can be done.
From windows all up and down our block, the round
bright faces of children peer out like flames.

**5** *Arrivals*

I enter the trees, a last mile,
wobblingly convinced
by appearances.
Nothing will arrest me now
that Mars is up and my path
tight and clear as a signal
on a thorn. I have only to go on
rending the seams of my fearful
nature. I have only to beast
when beast must be.

That's the way.

One step and then another step
before you know. All must proceed
into the flexing shadow, heaven
of lost gloves and pencil ends.
It is useless to struggle. Mute assemblages
of moss
wait for more moss, everyone.

That's the way.

Praise for rough roads in their certain
interminable consequence.
That glow in the homey window,
when we finally arrive, turns out
is the house afire.

## A CHRISTMAS ODE AFTER THE FASHION OF MICHAEL
## HEFFERNAN AND DEDICATED TO HIM AND HIS BRIDE

Rilke believed in an immortal essence to which one returned
by means of transformation, such as that the poet will
sometimes ignite, flying "beyond all substance"
like a surprised and flaming angel made of strophes and little bells.
It was a child-is-father-of-the-man
sort of thing and a continuing accomplishment of sheerest faith
in the Cheshire vicissitudes of art. And I'll not deny
that in spite of deceits and mockeries I myself have lived
and given over into speech, at times
when laboring at my staves or rummaging in that room of the brain
that breeds them, I've felt the tidal surge of a sweetness reborn.
Last night, for instance, in my dream I held extensive and studied
conversation with my cat who was strong for the undeniability
of Prime Cause as a sort of *Via Positiva* by which faith and all mortal
acts of conscience are set palpably free of mathematical oppressions.
"But how then," I wanted to know, "is Prime Cause established
as over against circularities of the Taoists, and others, who insist
primacy is eternal completion, the one life clapping,
so to speak?" I put this civilly enough, and he acknowledging
through the milk that was clinging to his whiskers said, "Ah, but
are we not born? Is not each belighted instant the creation *restored*
so that Prime Cause is shown us and in us always, our very
longings the proof of grace—and grace proof of the ineffable hand?"
And as I was lighting my pipe to consider this
a garbage truck burst into the room and flattened him like an old hat
and I woke with missing him so profoundly I went out
scantily into the snow and brought him from under the porch
and set him a bowl of turkey drippings on the moon-bathed floor
and said, "Certainly you're right, Prime Cause is clear as night from dawn,"
which had him purring with wonder at my transformation, so long
in coming, so home-like and easy at the dark edge of day.

# ALL DAY AT THE BRAINARD PIONEER CEMETERY

I

It is said of grief
it dwindles
with time, like a suitcase
carried slowly off down the road
by a blind man.
But what if my blind man stumbles,
sits down on the battered
blue belt-strapped bag
and lights a cigarette
with one of the black flames
which leak from his eyes and fly up
like angels?
What if he brings his face
into his hands and says it's no use,
his shoes are broken,
the sun wants him dead and the bag
is so dense with grief's amazement
I'll have to carry it myself?

## II

It is not night at all,
nor the shadow of a bird,
only my own
shadow tracing the chiseled letters,
dropping the roses and collecting them again
like pieces of a story, like shoes.
Rhinestones
shine in the cracked blue sockets
of dusk's teacup.
Nearby
King David cries, "Absalom, Absalom,"
letting all arrogance and time
go, letting history take what it wants
and get out.
Around us, in the vanished fields
and farms, ghost horses plod
in their enormous quiet
and birdsong turns to bare fingers
of the winter trees.

"I will lift up mine eyes unto the hills,"
sings the minstrel whose harp brought Saul
to tears. So I, too, lift up mine eyes, following
all the empty roads, turning out
my pockets, casting off my shoes that brim
with cold.
"From whence cometh my help?" he cries
and all the living
and the dead are listening to know.

Among rotting apples and the tilted stones,
I and this old king in the gold
of our brokenness
call out, "My child, my child,
how can this be?"

**III**
Trouble is

we've all come home at once
and the smoke of an absence there
is deafening our blossoms.

Did I say something grand
to an hourglass?
Did she come through the indigo hedge

of that far burning other
shore? Either way, quiet as a name
I'm handing out the cold

that keeps us walking.
Quiet as the cold star sister
in my window, done

with loneliness
I'm rocking a little tower
of leaves. Red and precious

who knows why
or how to live in these
empty rooms, but I remember

what love is
and hold on to that.

## COLE PORTER

The fisherman stands as always
between dark and what may be
the shore
and of course his line is out
but since the shape of time is namelessness
and time and matter are as Einstein says
intra-indicated
the question may be who will reel in who
not when
and it is clear for instance that nothing is
causal except in that one thing
follows another, evening and afternoon
are words.
                            In the trees nearby a shower
of woodchips sprays up from the twinkling axe
and the sound of its bite strolls off to where
the Lord is
musing about plywood
and the loneliness brought to pass
so beyond all healing possibility
if I pray He listens
and gives me a soft little sock on the arm and arranges
as a gesture those
beautiful entanglings of shadow
the moon makes climbing through bare alder boughs
just the way Saint Bernard saw and praised it
as he lay down in his cold stream to unwrap the gift
of Faith with what he called Reason
though it may have been only what he wanted
and not what he knew that brought him strength
and sleep.

                Oh teach me to glimmer
the wise man prays
or teach me to stay like the fisherman
alone
                all night waiting for the sea
that has no mother
that rocks and keens in mourning for its own
spacious music that gives then
takes away.

## KEATS

When Keats, at last beyond the curtain
of love's distraction, lay dying in his room
on the Piazza di Spagna, the melody of the Bernini
Fountain "filling him like flowers,"
he held his breath like a coin, looked out
into the moonlight and thought he saw snow.
He did not suppose it was fever or the body's
weakness turning the mind. He thought, "England!"
and there he was, secretly, for the rest
of his improvidently short life: up to his neck
in sleigh bells and the impossibly English cries
of street vendors, perfect
and affectionate as his soul.
For days the snow and statuary sang him so far
beyond regret that if now you walk rancorless
and alone there, in the Piazza, the white shadow
of his last words to Severn, "Don't be frightened,"
may enter you.

# LIKE RAIN DESCENDING

Out of blackness rain dives down
like diamonds
into the new grass, into "the beautiful
uncut hair of graves," as Whitman called it.
Across eternity's light-drenched miles I imagine
my father, after long hours in the garden,
beckoning the angels by sighing
in his happy weariness. I think
folds of shadow under the rhododendron
are suffused with mystifications
so delicate the blossoms nearly speak,
though they know this would be wrong.
I think of serious and painful solace,
my sinews and bones strumming
a little tune when they open and admit
the fast falling dark cheekbone
of an ending. I think of numbers
set free in a huge bowl and Fabergé
weeping on the last train out
of St. Petersburg. I think of chastity
and kissing and the smile
of a Portuguese dwarf who once sold me
a watch when I needed the exact
betrayal, blades blinking in the leaves
and vice versa. Something with wings
departs and someone says, "Don't touch
the broken spots," but I do and my father
is like rain descending into the clarity
of darkness thinking of light, thinking
of what must be love's long embrace
and everything and no one enduring it.

## THE NEW ORPHEUS
*—for Emma (1981–2001)*


As though windows had been nailed shut
I look out at the blank insides
of my eyes. Who lives here
in fire so deep it loves the water?
A handful of shells and a peacock moon
lie down in the dark of my arm.
Pins and needles, sorrow and salt: I'm trying
hard to match things up
with their Platonic other shinings.
I need more time for this
place I need to open like a door of rain,
like everything coming down
because of blue saturations of the unforgettable
and too hard to know. I'm giving myself just one
more lifetime of prying and pulling
at my hinges, beating the old empty roses
my daughter walks in, thinking I've been away
too long now, it's getting late, they're slamming
the other world and dousing the lights.
Rain and rain again, old winter. It's really dark
where she is. All night I lie awake
building a ladder of light.

## HEAVEN

So come home
along the dusty hickory-shaded ruts
with scotch broom ablaze
and orchards rising behind the sharp green
of berry fields. Come on ahead
if you can, with your fractures and played out
luck, your shoes that have forgotten
and had to be carried.
Come with steel-colored hair and slivers
of music half embedded in your heavy arms.
Did you think they would know you
topping the rise, smiling in so much
quiet it must be Sunday here
but it isn't? Did you suppose Jesus
here, too, suffering the little children,
preaching to the hill?
Whatever you thought, come on
having got so far, having found permission
for this finally-blue-again sky, dense
with robins and their singing.
The ice man's here, and the occasional horse
before a plough
and men and women who've risen
and walked here happily all their lives
and who've had so little but this happiness
they can't imagine why you've been away.

# ACKNOWLEDGMENTS

Poems in the "New" section originally appeared in journals as follows:

*The American Literary Review:* "Love Calls Us to the Things of the Other World"
*Basalt:* "July," "Unaccountable"
*Bellingham Review:* "The Mysterious Courtesy of Fondness"
*Burnside Review:* "Dancers"
*Crazyhorse:* "Marsh," "Another Letter to the Soul"
*Field:* "Jung Doubts"
*The Gettysburg Review:* "Letting Things Go," "The 'President' Speaks Out on the Issues," "Dust to Dust," "At Midnight," "Visitation," "Burning Bush"
*Hanging Loose:* "The Hot Corner"
*Hubbub:* "Desperados"
*The Journal:* "Circles in the Shell of the Ear," "Face," "Home Is the Sailor, "I have Wasted My Life"
*The Kerf:* "The Radio was Playing Strauss," "Time Travel"
*The Lyric Review:* "Mercy"
*The Southern Review,* "Something Borrowed," "The New Creation"
*Turnrow:* "Tiger Tiger"

*Decomposition,* ed. Chadwick and Roehl, Lost Horse Press, Sandpoint, ID, 2010: "Letting Things Go"
*Poets of the American West*, ed. Lowell Jaeger, Many Voices Press, Kalispell, MT, 2010: "Burning Bush," "Desperados"

Poems from those collections herein included appeared in:

*The American Literary Review, The Antioch Review, Ascent, Black Warrior Review, California Quarterly, The Chadakoin Review, The Chicago*

*Review, The Cimmaron Review, Clackamas Literary Review, The Connecticut
Review, Crazyhorse, The Denver Quarterly, FIELD, Fine Madness, Fireweed,
Flint Hills Review, The Gettysburg Review, The Green Mountains Review,
Harper's, The Hollins Critic, Hubbub, Hudson Review, The Iowa Review,
Ironwood, Local Earth, Massachusetts Review, The Midwest Quarterly,
The Minnesota Review, Mississippi Mud, The Mississippi Review, The New
Orleans Review, The North American Review, The Northwest Review, Poetry
Northwest, The Portland Review, Redactions, Smackwarm, Southern Poetry
Review, Sou'wester, Willow Springs*

In addition to having appeared in the full-length volumes named in the
text, some of the poems in this book appeared in the following limited
edition collections:

*The Bear in the Mirror,* Raincrow Press (Cincinnati, OH), 1977
*Red Alders in an Island Dream,* Trask House Books (Portland, OR), 1980
*The Jetty,* Clatsop Community College (Astoria, OR), 1982
*The Wu General Writes from far Away,* Black Oak Press (Petersham, MA),
 1990
*King of the Butterflies,* The Brady Press (Omaha, NE), 2003

Additionally, some of these poems were anthologized in the following
volumes:

*Decomposition*, Lost Horse Press, Sandpoint, ID, 2010
*Poets of the American West,* Many Voices Press, Kalispel, MT, 2009
*Poet's Calendar,* Alhambra Press, Bruges, Belgium, 2009
*Breathe: 101 Contemporary Odes,* C & R Press, Chatanooga, TN, 2009
*Zeus Seduces the Wicked Stepmother . . . ,* Winterhawk Press, Boise, ID, 2008
*Poet's Calendar,* Alhambra Press, Bruges, Belgium, 2007
*Long Journey: Contemporary Northwest Poets,* Oregon State University Press,
 Corvallis, OR, 2006
*Poet's Calendar,* Alhambra Press, Bruges, Belgium, 2006
*180 More Extraordinary Poems for Everyday*, Random House, NYC, 2005
*A Range of Voices,* Eastern Washington University Press, Cheney, WA, 2005

*Red, White, and Blues,* University of Iowa Press, Iowa City, IA, 2004

*Sea of Voices, Isle of Story,* Triple Tree Publications, Eugene, OR, 2003

*March Hares,* Fine Madness, Seattle, WA, 2003

*The Pushcart Prize: Best of the Small Presses XXVII,* Pushcart Press, Wain-
scott, NY, 2003

*The Pushcart Prize: Best of the Small Presses XXIV,* Pushcart Press,
Wainscott, NY, 2000

*Dog Music,* St. Martin's Press, NYC, 1996

*From Here We Speak,* Oregon State University Press, Corvallis, OR, 1993

*A New Geography of Poets,* University of Arkansas Press, Fayetteville, AR,
1992

*A Gathering of Poets,* Kent State University Press, Kent, OH, 1992

*Deep Down Things: Poems of the Inland Pacific Northwest,* Washington State
University Press, Pullman, WA, 1990

*Anthology of Magazine Verse & Yearbook of American Poetry,* Monitor Books,
Beverly Hills, CA, 1988

*Crossing the River,* The Permanent Press, Sag Harbor, NY, 1987

*Carrying the Darkness: The Poetry of the Vietnam War,* Avon Books, NY, 1985

*Anthology of Magazine Verse & Yearbook of American Poetry,* Monitor Books,
Beverly Hills, CA, 1985

*Rain in the Forest, Light in the Trees,* Owl Creek Press, Missoula, MT, 1983

*The Pushcart Prize: Best of the Small Presses III,* Yonkers, NY, 1978

*The Islanders,* Vashon Allied Arts, Vashon, WA, 1978


Special thanks are due to Linda Bierds, Christopher Buckley, Bill Tremblay,
Albert Goldbarth, Richard Morgan, Melissa Kwasny, Tony Flinn, Christine
Holbert, and David Luckert for the years of care, wisdom, and support.
I wish to thank also my fine colleagues and students at Eastern Washington
University's Inland NW Center for Writers for forging and maintaining
a community where art is practiced, valued, and understood.


Acknowledgment is also due the Eastern Washington University Scholar-
ship and Creativity Committee for the fellowship that allowed me the time
and psychological space necessary to assemble this volume.

And finally, many thanks to Ashley Saleeba, Marilyn Trueblood, Alice Herbig, Gretchen Van Meter, and Pat Soden of the University of Washington Press for their thoughtful and professional treatment of me and my work.

## ABOUT THE POET

© MATTHEW VALENTINE

**CHRISTOPHER HOWELL** has published nine books of poetry, including *Just Waking* (2003) and *Light's Ladder* (2004). He has received two Washington State Book Awards, two National Endowment for the Arts fellowships, a fellowship from Artist Trust, and the Vachel Lindsay and Helen Bullis prizes. His work has made several appearances in the annual *Pushcart Prize* publication and may be found in many journals and anthologies. He is professor of English and Creative Writing at Eastern Washington University. He lives in Spokane.

## A NOTE ON THE TYPE

The poems are set in 10.3 pt. Hoefler Text with 15.5 pt. leading. Hoefler Text was designed in 1991 by Jonathan Hoefler. The poem titles are set in 10 pt. Gotham Medium. Gotham was designed in 2000 by Hoefler & Frere-Jones. Typesetting is by Ashley Saleeba.